AF540624

ENVIRONMENTAL AWARENESS AND SECONDARY STUDENTS

ENVIRONMENTAL AWARENESS AND SECONDARY STUDENTS

By

Dr. Shivakumar, G.S.

M.Sc., M.Ed.

Assistant Professor

Deptt. of Education

Kumadvathi College of Education

Shikaripura (Karnataka)

(India)

DISCOVERY PUBLISHING HOUSE PVT. LTD.

NEW DELHI-110 002

Published by:
Tilak Wasan

DISCOVERY PUBLISHING HOUSE PVT. LTD.
4383/4B, Ansari Road, Darya Ganj
New Delhi-110 002 (India)
Phone : +91-11-23279245, 43596064-65
Fax : +91-11-23253475
E-mail : parul.wasan@gmail.com
discoverypublishinghouse@gmail.com
web : www.discoverypublishinggroup.com

***First Edition:* 2013**

ISBN: 978-93-5056-261-1

Environmental Awareness and Secondary Students

Printed at:
Dynamic Printers
Delhi

Preface

Environmental education aims at raising the sensitivity and awareness of learners towards their surroundings and also to inculcate proper habits and positive attitudes towards the environment. One of the single most important drivers of environmental change in the future will be the environmental awareness and attitudes of people in this country and abroad. Environmental awareness influences individual behavior, and individual behavior is a fundamental factor affecting environmental conditions.

Environmental education is an essential part of every pupil's curriculum. It helps to encourage awareness of the environment, leading to informed concern for and active participation in resolving environmental problems. Objectives of environmental education is to increase the public awareness of the problems in this field, as well as possible solutions, and to lay the foundations for a fully informed and active participation of individual in the protection of the environment and the prudent and rational use of the natural resources.

The long term aims of environmental education are to improve management of the environment and provide satisfactory solutions to environmental issues and also it is a process that aims at the development of environmentally literate citizens those who can compete in global economy, those who have the skills and knowledge and inclinations to make well informed choices concerning the Environment.

Environmental education must become a vehicle for engaging young minds in the excitement of first hand observation of the nature and understanding the patterns and processes in the natural and social worlds.

In view of the deteriorating environment that we encounter today, there is a great need for highlighting the importance of safeguarding children's health through promotion of healthy environment. As is known, every year millions of children die from environmental disasters. These children could be saved by creating healthy environs, be it at the home, the school or the community of which they are an integral part. Environmental Education will create awareness among children and facilitate their growth in a healthy home, school and community. One cannot dispute the fact that Environmental Education will serve as a springboard for raising awareness, stimulating debate and building the momentum for a national movement that tackles health risks in places where children live, learn and play. Environmental Education will enable every child to grow up in a healthy home, school and community. In fact, the future development of our children, and, of course, their world depends on their enjoying good health. For this to take place, however, the Environmental Education teachers need to be properly equipped with not only updated knowledge on environment but also effective strategies of teaching to drive home the message of environmental protection and conservation among the students.

Modern developmental processes enabled humans to exploit natural resources indiscriminately. Forests, minerals, water, air and land have been meeting the needs of humans since time immemorial. While depending on these resources, somewhere in history, humans have lost the capacity of natural regeneration. Increasing rates of consumption led to faster depletion of resources.

The key to successful implementation of Environmental Education is the classroom teacher. For it is the teacher, who, in the ultimate analysis, interprets and implements Environmental Education in the classroom. Given this central role of teacher in any educational process, teacher education at both the preservice and in-service levels becomes vital.

The mental and physical aspects of child are related to more heredity and less environment. The social, cultural and emotio-nal aspects are influenced by the environment. The education has to play the very significant role for providing the awareness, developing skills, attitudes and values of student at various levels.

Emergence of environmental education as a compulsory subject at school level is a welcome subject. India can protect and restore environmental and natural resources by spreading awareness on such issues among its citizens.

In this book the author has discussed about various aspects of environment and their relationship with gender and locality in order to highlight the dimensions of the environmental awareness, environmental attitude and environmental knowledge among secondary school students. He has substantiated his discussions by empirical data collected on a sample of secondary students selected from 36 secondary schools of Davangere district in Karnataka state.

The study has lead to the dimensions of environmental awareness, environmental attitude and environmental knowledge among the secondary school students. The author has offered some valuable suggestions or recommendations for taking remedial measures on the basis of research findings.

I owe my deepest gratitude to my esteemed Guide Dr. H.S. Jayappa, Professor (Retd.), S J V P college of Education, Harihar and Co-Guide Dr. H.V. Vmamadevappa, Professor and Research Guide, M M college of Education, Davangere and Dr. D.S. Shivananda, Professor (Retd.), Bangalore University, Bangalore for their able guidance and constant encouragement.

I am grateful to Discovery publishing House, New Delhi for taking keen interest to make the book the best.

This book will be of great use to teachers and researchers of Education and all those concerned with planning policy making and development of Education in India.

Dr. Shivakumar, G.S.

Acknowledgement

The author expresses his most sincere and heartfelt gratitude to his esteemed guide, Dr.H.S.Jayappa and Dr. H.V. Vamadevappa. visiting professors, Department of P.G. Studies in Education and Research, Kuvempu University, Jnanasahyadri, Shankaraghatta, Shimogha for their valuable guidance, inspiring suggestions and the keen interest evinced by them in the successful completion of this research work.

The author expresses his indelible indebtedness and deep sense of gratitude to Dr. D.S. Shivananda, Ph.D. Ex-Principal, Sarvagna College of Education, Bangalore, whose constant inspiration and valuable suggestions at every stage of this research have enabled me to complete this investigation.

The author is grateful to the Secretary, Director and Administrator SVVS trust, Shikaripura as well as Dr. Jayashree, V.R. Principal, Kumadvathi College of Education, Shikaripura and my other colleagues for their whole hearted support and co-operation in successful completion of this work.

The author is also grateful to Dr. S.S.Patil, Dean and Chairman, Department of P.G, Studies in Education, Kuvempu University, Jnana shyadri, Shankaraghatta, Shimoga for his valuable moral support.

The author is grateful to Prof. Sangam, J.J.M. Medical College, Davangere for the help rendered by him in analysing the data and in providing computer facilities for the analysis.

The author is thankful to the Head Masters / Head Mistress and 9th standard students of selected secondary school of Davangere District for their whole hearted support and co-operation during the collection of the data for the study. The author expresses his sincere thanks to Sri. Dayanand, Y.M. Librarian, B.E.A, College of Education for having extended his help in providing of library facilities.

The author's heart felt thanks are due to his wife Smt, Usha. M.S, whose painstaking efforts in scoring of the answer scripts with me have enabled to complete the work well in time.

I express my deep gratitude to my parents Sri M.G. Siddabasappa and Smt. Gangamma, G.P and daughter Shravya, G.S. for their co-operation, encouragement and help.

Finally I thank all my well-wishers, family members and friends specially Dinesh and Kalmesh for their constant concern, encouragement and constant criticism.

Shiv Kumar, G.S.

Contents

1

Introduction

Background of the Study

Today man is living in a world of crises. The social, economic, political and value crises are some of the threats which are quite alarming. Added to this, in the recent decades, the environmental crisis has become another important factor that has made everyone in the world to think of its gravity. Ever since man has been on this earth, there has been a constant interaction between him and the natural world. In the beginning man lived in harmony with nature, but as his numbers grew and his scientific discoveries and inventions led him on the path of industrialization, he became the predator and his increasing demands on the environment and its resources has led to its exploitation and degradation. The role of education in understanding, protecting and solving problems related to environment has been realized all over the world since 1970.

Today environmental problems are matter of concern. The very survival of man depends on the solution of these problems. Awareness is essential for action and education can play a vital role in this direction. It is education which can make man aware, conscious of and knowledgeable about environment and environmental problems. (18:3-5)

Over the last quarter of a century, environmental education has been a widely discussed and highly politicized cross- curricular area in most of the countries. Environment and nature study programs were thus intended to equip children with moral and spiritual insights. These were to be initiated through early casual acquaintance, observation, and curiosity, leading towards the aesthetic enjoyment of nature, and hence not only to an effectual response to environment but also to the development of a self-reliant, morally brave and wholesomely humble character.(25:6-29)

Environmental education promotes good science, serious debate, and thoughtful action. Environmental education engages the student's minds and hands, often in real-world investigations that are inquiry based, interdisciplinary, and supportive of a standard-based curriculum. (2) Environmental education also familiarizes the students with career in environmental fields. Career opportunities related to environmental protection range from manual labor to high-tech jobs. (9)

Environmental education can help redress the significant source of skilled jobs with good pay for low -income persons and also the process of creating an integrated environment based curriculum heightened the professional team spirit of the schools teachers. Environmental education has long been seen by many teachers as an add that is difficult to fit into a crowded schedule. (3)

The environment in which the children live and plays an important role in which the acquisition of environmental concepts and there by an environmental attitude develops in children.(19:21-26) The goal of environmental education is to develop a world population that is aware of, and concerned about, the environmental and its associated problems, and which has the knowledge, skills, attitudes, motivations and commitment to work individually and collectively toward solutions of current problems and the prevention of new ones. (4)

Further, environmental education is rooted in the belief that humans can live compatibly with nature, humans can act equally towards each other, human well being is inextricably bound with environmental quality, we and the systems we create-our societies, political systems, economics, religions, cultures, technologies impact the total environment.

Environmental pollution has become a world wide problem. In eradicating environmental pollution, the programs conducted should study the level of awareness and attitude of the target group. Among the many strategies suggested by psychologists, the study of attitude remains an important one. In changing the attitude of the masses towards environmental pollution, environmental education plays a major role. (22:34-36)

The main objective of introducing the environmental studies in school curriculum is to help children to acquire a set of values and feelings of concern for the environment and motivation for feelings of concern for the environment and motivation for activity participating in environmental improvement and protection. (21:21-26)

The objectives of environmental education is to provide the individual and social groups sufficient scope so that they should acquire awareness and knowledge, develop attitudes, skills and abilities, and participation in solving real–life environmental problems. The perspective should be integrated following an interdisciplinary approach, and should be holistic in nature. The important objective of environmental education is therefore not to introduce a new subject but to evolve a new approach to education to integrate the concept of preserving environment with the existing content of a subject–discipline. Hence environmental education is an approach, which is expected to provide the necessary methodology to integrate the consciousness about environment.

The role of younger generation is crucial in achieving these objectives. Hence it is necessary to know about the awareness of younger generations about environment and environmental problems. In these present studies, the researcher has made an attempt to analyze the environmental awareness, attitude and knowledge among secondary school students of different localities.

Genesis of the Problem

Limitless greed, reckless consumption of natural resources and unkind treatment meted out to environment has increasingly damaged the world. The earth is fast losing its treasures. The soil we cultivate, the water we drink and the air we breathe are all polluted. This has caused a global concern about the conservation and protection of the earth's environment. A number of world conferences have emphasised the need for generating, through education, awareness and sensitivity towards this alarming situation in order to protect the environment. (12)

The unprecedented increase in population and intensity of human activities, which have occurred largely in this century, has been brought about by the growing mastery of science and its application. This has produced prosperity, improved standards of life and expanded opportunities beyond what earlier generations could have imagined. But these developments have damaged and deteriorated the ecological systems and caused widespread destruction of natural resources base, on which human life and well being depended. The co-operation of world's people is essential to mitigate or avert these environmental risks. Students constitute a major portion of our community. Therefore students participation is essential in any program. (20: 25-26).

The planet, earth is the only place in the whole universe where mankind can live. We need to take care of it. Today developing and developed countries are facing severe and serious environmental problems. We not only face environmental problems but also create them. Our environment has an effect on us and is affected by us. For example, our cities are warm during night unlike the villages.

This is due to the large concrete buildings, which store heat from the sun. At night, as the air begins to cool, the buildings give off the heat. In addition, pollutants in the air around us create heat. Hence cities take long time to cool off. The quality of our life depends on 3p's namely pollution, poverty and population. Among the 3p's population is the main problem that affects the environment. Population leads to poverty, unemployment and pollution. (23:5-13)

Rapid degradation of environment quality is the most hazardous event of this century. Generally there is misconception that it is the responsibility of polluting industries alone to take care of the environment. No doubt, they need to be cautious about controlling industrial pollution, but that is not the end of the process. The population explosion causes a greater need for more food, more energy and more things of daily use such as housing, clothing and automobiles. As a result there is an increase in the use of water resources, fertilizers and pesticides for more production which in turn increases the level of all sorts of pollution besides disturbing the ecological balance in the ecosystem. Among other factors, degradation of environment and depletion of resources are caused by improper disposal of domestic and other wastes. This is due to lack of awareness about the need for preservation and conservation of environment. There is an urgent need to create environmental awareness among the people in respect of protection, preservation and conservation of environment.

India is a unique country with great cultural diversity, associated with all kinds of climates and rich flora and fauna. Living in harmony with nature has always been emphasised with the philosophy to take from nature only what we actually need and not more. We must conserve resources for our future generations. The sums of physical, chemical factors to which we are exposed constitute our environment. Today environmental education is an important segment with in the educational system. It includes all educational activities consciously confronting and attempting to overcome the environmental crisis. The objective of environmental education is to acquire awareness and knowledge, develop attitudes, skills and abilities to participate in solving real life environmental problems. Environmental learning is learning about the factors, causes and solutions to the environmental crisis.

Man faces physical, emotional, religious, economic and vocational problems in his entire life. Also he faces environmental problems. He disturbs the ecological balance due to his wrong practices such as explosion of population, production and consumption pattern causing stress and strain on natural resources affecting the life support systems. Aversion, attitude of conquest, desire, religious fundamentalism are some of traits of mind pollution which lead to war, inturn war produces pollution, poverty, sickness and so on. We can erase the pollution in mind with the help of values. The teaching and learning of academic disciplines needs to be informed by the concerns and values of environmental responsibility; peaceful use of energy; avoidance of pollution of air, water and soil, conservation of flora and fauna and ecological sustainability.

Over the past two centuries human development has taken place in leaps and bounds. But along with enormous growth in science and technology, man has brought brutal and catastrophic changes in our environment. Environmental protection has been neglected. There by all the progress what ever developed do not posses human face. It has been only during the past few decades that an awareness of the need for a harmonious relationship with the Nature has become concretized. The importance of environmental education for creating environmental awareness and responsibilities towards environmental protection for ecological balance, in the responsibilities towards environment has been considered in NPE 1986 and POA 1992 of India. It is certainly praise worthy to make the children aware about the environment and cultivate a healthy attitude and responsibility among them for the protection of environment through education to check the rapid resources deterioration of the present day.

The difficulties faced by developing countries like India, in reconciling today's environmental imperative with the need for economic growth can be turned to positive effect and the two can become self reinforcing with the environmental education. It is important to consider about how to increase attention and resources for implementing environmental education, communication and training and to achieve a balance between environmental and development constraints. Industrialization and urbanization led to massive depletion of natural resources and environmental pollution on a wide scale in developing countries. Over recent decades, global problems related to degradation of natural resources and to pollution have increased dramatically.

Natural resources are depleted by excessive use. Fresh water scarcity on a global scale, deforestation, degradation of coastal and marine ares, soil depletion and loss of bio-diversity are just some of the instances. Air and water pollution, in particular mega cities, has reached levels that are already giving rise to serious human health problems, as well as to negative impact on the environment, inevitably influencing prospects for long term economic growth. The handling and disposal of solid waste is now a major issue. (6:35-37)

Natural and physical environment influences man's physical and mental health directly. For the welfare of man, the study of environment is a dire necessity to maintain proper environment for the physical as well as mental health of a man. If he neglects environment, man's life will be in danger. So, environmental education should be encouraged to protect environment through formal and non formal education and to educate the people to save the environment.

Good physical environment and social environment decide the quality of life. While physical environment is highly stressed; the social environment is being neglected. Strangely enough, there has been a gradual erosion of ethical and moral values. Proper utilization of environment, protection and nourishment are needed for the healthy life of the population. Then one can at least control pollution. (13)

Hence there is a paramount need to create a consciousness of the environment. It must permeate all ages and all sections of society, beginning with the child. Environmental consciousness aspect must be integrated in the entire educational process. (21:30-44)

Need and Importance of the Study

The environment refers to sum total of all the conditions and influences that affect the life and development of organisms. The qualitative development and quantitative progress of man kind depends on the quality of the environment. Therefore there are no two views about the fact that, it is the primary responsibility of man not only to preserve the environment but also to improve it qualitatively. (10:10)

Environmental awareness is most important because people in developed countries are rapidly consuming earth's natural resources and world population is increasing rapidly. Hence Human beings must take individual and social responsibility for the environment. (8)

It is pathetic to notice that younger generation of India is much behind in the concern for environmental balance. Therefore it is felt need to study the environmental awareness, attitude and knowledge among the secondary school students. (5)

It is very important to raise awareness among the teaching and student community. The awareness raising programmes are mostly concentrated around certain areas and the rest of the country is left out. Preparing the teaching community for effective integration of environmental concepts and creating positive attitudes in the young minds are greatly needed in every strata of the educational system. Unfortunately, the present efforts get diluted in the mad rush for academic achievements. (18:3-5)

In the formal system of education followed in our schools, the environmental education aspect attracts low prioritization and is still treated as an 'extra curricular activity', despite the efforts of various governmental and non-governmental bodies to infuse the necessary environmental values. The follow-up programmes are also not being carried out regularly due to the difficulty in organizing programmes for the same group. (20:225-230) from the available literature and reports, it is evident that many governmental and non-governmental agencies are taking up many measures in educating the masses on environmental matters.

The National Curriculum for Elementary and Secondary Education-a framework formulated in 1988 (NCERT, 1988) marked the first concerted and systematic effort to bring environmental education into the school curriculum. This took the form of an infusion of environmental concerns, i.e., the introduction of descriptions of environmental problems and suggested solutions into existing subjects, primarily physical and social sciences. A whole range of environmental concerns was thus infused into the NCERT model textbooks published between 1987 and 1989. (16)

In 1987 the Ministry of Human Resources Development also announced a scheme, Environmental Orientation to School Education to support innovative work in the field of environmental education. Under this scheme a number of non-government organizations have experimented with various approaches to environmental education. (12) The programmes implemented by the government and non-governmental agencies lack coordination. The approach of the government in educating the masses is not directly linked with the school community. As a result, the efforts to create awareness among school children through various programmes get watered down in due course.(12:11-14)

Environmental education has been recognized all over the world as a viable tool for creating environmental awareness in people and motivating them to act for the environment. With the acceptance of Tiwari Committee Report in 1990, the country realized the need of environmental education. It is needed in order to meet the demand of every day life and maintain a mental equilibrium for the fulfillment of the needs and wants of every citizen on earth, and for balance and harmony between humanity and environment. It helps in developing new knowledge, skills and values in a drive towards better quality of life. It is needed for biomedical awareness and solution to health problems. A properly guided awareness is necessary to instill and enlighten the mind of Indians. Awareness leads to action. Without proper educational efforts the awareness analysis action chain does not move smoothly and effectively. (21:30-44)

It is usually accepted that if the present trend of environmental imbalance continues unchecked, it will lead to annihilation of living beings from this planet. (10:11-14) The main focus of environmental education programs is to change environmental behavior through increasing environmental awareness, attitude and knowledge. As many environmental studies have failed to apply successfully attitude theory in researching environmental attitudes, hence the present study investigates the awareness, attitude and knowledge among the secondary school students. Considering the aforesaid lacunae in

Environmental awareness, attitude and knowledge the investigator decided to take up the present study.

Environmental issues have been steadily occupying the international policy agenda for the past several years. Acid rain, desertification, global warming, ozone layer depletion, pollution of air, water and soil, radioactive contamination of large areas and species extinction are some of the most urgent environmental threats to be dealt with at present and in the future.

Around the world there are several crises- there is an environmental crisis, an energy crisis, a food crisis and a population crisis. There is intense competition among growing populations for limited resources. Modern industrial and economic growth was fueled by abundant resources, obtained either domestically or from less developed countries in Asia and Africa. Natural resource consumption patterns vary widely, the affluent consume a grossly disproportionate share of the world's resources. It is estimated that doubling of living standards in rich countries would increase the consumption of world resources six times as much as doubling of population in poor countries. High levels of consumption of natural resources are leading to depletion. Forests considered as carbon sinks of the world, are shrinking, particularly rain forests. (6:35-37)

India faces significant challenges in protecting the environment from further damage. Population growth and urbanization make the task all the more difficult for the Indian government. It has made significant efforts in the field of environmental protection, and developing environmental standards for both products and processes. The Indian government's ability to safeguard the countries environment depends on polices and educational systems. The quality of life of people living in urban areas has declined considerably because of pollution. Protection of the environment is one of the major challenges facing the world. Hence human beings are asked to reduce, reuse and recycle their resources. Even the learned people do not know which object are to be reduced, reused and recycled. These three words if followed each and every person would be helpful to protect our environment.

Statement of the Problem

The problem of the present investigation is –*"An Investigation into the Environmental Awareness, Attitude and Knowledge among the Secondary School Students of Davangere District"*

Objectives of the Study

The present study was undertaken with the following broad objectives:

(*i*) To identify the environmental awareness among the secondary school students

(*ii*) To identify the environmental attitude among the secondary school students.

(*iii*) To identify the environmental knowledge among the secondary school students.

(*iv*) To suggest measures to develop environmental awareness, attitude and knowledge among the secondary school students of Davangere District

Specific Objectives of the Study

(*a*) To find out the environmental awareness among the secondary school Boys and Girls of Davangere District.

(*b*) To find out the environmental awareness among the Rural and Urban Secondary school Boys and Girls of Davangere District.

(*c*) To find out the environmental awareness among the secondary school Boys and Girls of Government and Private secondary schools of Davangere District.

(*d*) To find out the environmental Attitude among the secondary school Boys and Girls of Davangere District.

(*e*) To find out the environmental Attitude among the Rural and Urban Secondary school Boys and Girls of Davangere District.

(*f*) To find out the environmental Attitude among the secondary school Boys and Girls of Government and Private secondary schools of Davangere District.

(*g*) To find out the environmental knowledge among the secondary school Boys and Girls of Davangere District.

(*h*) To find out the environmental knowledge among the Rural and Urban Secondary school Boys and Girls of Davangere District.

(*i*) To find out the environmental knowledge among the secondary School Boys and Girls of Government and Private secondary schools of Davangere District.

(*j*) To find out the interaction effect of Sex and Locality on Environmental awareness, attitude and knowledge of secondary school students.

(*k*) To find out the interaction effect of Sex and Types of schools on Environmental awareness, attitude and knowledge of secondary school students.

(*l*) To find out the interaction effect of Locality and Types of school on Environmental awareness, attitude and knowledge of secondary school students.

Education and Environment

The role of education is to prepare young minds to appreciate the importance of environment in a holistic manner, not only for human survival but for all life forms on Earth, to inculcate a positive attitude towards environment, and to encourage pro-active action for a sustainable future. (24:4)

The overall objectives of environmental education is to develop in the learner an awareness of the environment and its problems, basic knowledge and understanding of the environment and its inter-relationship with man including indigenous tradition and cultural practices related to the environment. Habits, values, attitudes and emotions to maintain and promote quality environment for human survival. To attain skills to solve environmental problems, ability to assess the outcomes of environmental action and initiatives with a sense of responsibility and urgency to ensure appropriate action to solve environmental problems. (17:256-257)

At the secondary stage, the focus of environmental education as a compulsory subject should not mainly be on knowledge and information processing but on acquisition of skills, development of attitudes and values and participation in actions through activities, projects, field interactions and co-curricular activities. The school environment should be both a demonstration and a manifestation of the environmental education process. Environmental values have to be suitably integrated with the curriculum, teaching-learning process and teacher education. (18)

The efforts to educate ourselves about nature are a continuous and lifelong process. For the past few decades we have been trying to preserve and protect the natural resources through various means and measures. Even after so many years of talking about the environment, we have not achieved the desired results in conserving the natural resources. The intellectual arguments and international deliberations at various floras fail to yield tangible results. The reason may be attributed to many factors ranging from lack of commitment, low prioritization, exploitative culture, scarcity of economic resources, disparity in growth and distribution of resources. In short, the unsustainable way of life lacks fresh initiatives and a real concern for nature. (19)

It is a known fact that the growing population and ever increasing needs mount enormous pressure on the natural resources. To counter the pressure on natural resources, we must intensify our efforts to conserve the environment. Raising awareness among the people about the importance of the environment is vital and has to be a continuous and sustained process. In the same way, preparation of teachers and teacher educators also needs concentrated effort. The existing infrastructure and methods should be upgraded and intensified. (19) Environment is a good teaching aid and research studies have shown that learning through the environment facilitates better conceptual understanding. (7)

Education is the catalyst for the desire to live together in their own society on the one hand, and the global village on the other, through the teaching of universal values such as tolerance and human rights, the diversity of cultures, respect for others and for the environment by searching for the right balance between the society's concerns and the integrity of the individual. (1:36-40) Concern for preserving our environment for a sustainable development has been felt by all quarters. Education, particularly school education, could play a greater role by making an impact on the thinking of young minds to protect the universe from deterioration. (18)

There needs to be complete awareness of the total natural environment and its problems. The awareness must include being sensitive to possible and actual problems. Societies must develop the awareness. Social groups and individuals must achieve a basic understanding of the environment and discern which are major as well as minor problem areas to consider. A value system is required to indicate concern as well as participating in protecting and improving the environment. Knowledge must result in the use of skills to identify and solve problem areas. Active participation of individuals and groups are needed in working toward solutions to environmental problems. (14:17-19)

Environmental education has developed as pragmatic educational response to the problems and concerns of environment. The concept of environmental education is still evolving and awaiting institutionalization in the educational system. As such there is dire need to understand the subject in proper perspective. Environmental education has two components, viz., environmental education is the process of recognizing values and the clarifying concepts in order to develop the skill and attitudes necessary to understand and appreciate the interrelations among man, his culture and his biophysical surroundings.

Environmental education is an interdisciplinary process that equips people with the knowledge, attitudes, skills and motivation they need to help resolve environmental issues. Unlike the formal education, environmental education is aimed at effecting behavioral change. However, this definition is subject to enormous debate. Research in developed countries suggests that despite twenty or so years of environmental awareness and education, people have not substantially changed their value systems. This experience reveals the fact that knowledge acquired through environmental education should lead to change in people's values and attitudes. Thus environmental education is defined not by knowledge alone-it should foster a diversity of values, not only in the class room, but in society as well. (15)

Environmental education is valuable and necessary. Starting from a very young age, children should be taught about the environment that surrounds them. As they grow, their environmental awareness and knowledge of the area in which they live should grow. Their education should be sequential and integrated with core disciplines. In addition to a sound knowledge base, students should be taught critical thinking skills and recognize that they have the right to act on their beliefs if they choose. Environmental education includes science, maths, social science and language arts, Health and physical education.

The environmental education should be education, not advocacy. Environmental education should give information on 'actions'. But, responsible and informed action has been a goal of environmental education. Environmental education also emphasizes on personal and social decision making. Personal and social decision making is seen as ultimate goals of environmental education. Environmental education programmes must teach knowledge based on a balanced presentation of current scientific information. Media has a greater role in promoting environmental education. Basic environmental education provides the foundation for all future environmental education and learning. (11)

To protect the environment, environmental education is inevitable–education for the environment, education about the environment and education through the environment. So environmental education should be given more importance and be taught at different levels and different stages.

An important reason for linking environment and education is that environmental education can contribute significantly to transformation and development. Environmentally literate citizens are able to consider the ecological sustainability of development, to actively work to reverse environmental degradation, and to manage and use the countries natural resource base more wisely and democratically. They can use information, legislation, and community action to protect and improve human and environmental health. Environmental education also contributes to transformation through better education. (13)

Environmental education is a necessity to develop and maintain clean and sustainable air, land, and water habitats for life in its diverse forms. Pollution is common in society, and its effects are numerous. It behoves school to develop quality objectives. Learning opportunities, and evaluation procedures in environmental education to encourage students to become goods stewards of natural environment. The environment must be conserved to make quality living as well as for generations.

Environmental protection has not yet received the attention from citizens and the public policy on it will only be implemented succefully. If the citizens take up the issue in all its intensity. The solution to the present day environmental crisis does not lie either with the government or with the scientist but with a well educated citizenry. It is only an aware citizenry that can play a vital role in environmental preservation. The immediate issue is to replace shorter attitudes to environment which see it as a commodity to be exploited, with attitudes which look to sustainable rather than maximal level of progress and development. The route to the long term attitudes invariably is education. The media must, therefore, through its popular reach inform people about the environmental problems, relationship and help them to sort out facts from emotional rhetoric.

Environmental education should be to the desire of directing ones activities towards improving the quality of the environment. It should enable an individual to perceive and solve the existing problems. In this regard it is the school, colleges and universities which have a very important role to play as they contain a more mature class of students on the one hand and well developed faculties for research and development of environment on the other. They are also training grounds for both the future environmental experts who will deal with the problems in the field and future academicians who will be the teachers of environmental education in primary and secondary schools. But it is often becomes too difficult to achieve this multidisciplinary objective.

Scope of the Study

The present study has tried to study the environmental awareness, attitude and knowledge among the secondary school students of Davangere District. The investigator has tried to identify the environmental awareness, attitude and knowledge among the secondary school students and studied the relationship of the environmental awareness, attitude and knowledge among the Boys and Girls, Urban and Rural, Government and Private secondary school students of Davangere District.

The proposed study will be confined to the secondary school (9th standard) students presently studying in Davangere District as they will be in the middle of the secondary education. 8th standard students are fresh for high school education as they have come from primary education. They are lacking in the basic concepts of environment. Hence they are not selected as sample. Even 10th standard students are not selected as sample because they will be busy in preparing for the board examinations and also the lack of cooperation from the heads of the schools. Hence the sample covers randomly selected rural and urban secondary school (9th standard) students of Davangere District.

Resume of the Succeding Chapters

The research report is presented in five chapters. The chapter plan is as follows-Chapter I titled introduction, which deals with the background of the study which consists of genesis of the problem, need and importance of the study, statement of the problem and objectives of the study. It has also dealt with the education and the environment and scope of the problem.

Chapter II titled review of related literature, deals with the review of related studies which helped the researcher to design the present study. The reviews include the studies related to environmental awareness, attitude and knowledge among the students.

Chapter-III under the heading Methodology of the study, gives the details regarding selection of variables, discussion and definitions of variables and terms, hypotheses needed to be tested, description of the various tools used for the collection of data, sampling, administration and scoring of the test, and statistical techniques used for analysis of data.

Chapter- IV titled analysis and interpretation of data deals with analysis techniques, tables, figures and description of findings pertinent to each hypothesis. In this chapter, the research hypotheses set-up have been tested by using the test of significance of difference between the means and also by using Two way ANOVA.

Chapter-V titled summary of the findings and suggestions, deals with the brief summary of the earlier chapters, findings and conclusions of the study, educational implications of the study, and limitations of the study and suggestions for further research.

REFERENCES

1. Armstrong, J., & Impara, J: *"The Impact of an Environmental Education Programme on Knowledge and Attitude".* Journal of Environmental Education, 2 (4), 1991, pp.36-40.

2. Archi, M: "*Excellence in Environmental Education: Guidelines for Learning"* (K- 10). Washington, D C: *North American Association for Environmental Education.* 2009.
3. Archi, M: "*Five Years of Advancing Education and Environmental Literacy".* Washington, D.C: *North American Association for Environmental Education,* 2001.
4. Belgrade: *"Character Environmental Education Network".* Washington.D.C. NAEE, 1976.
5. Deshbandu: *"Environmental Education for Sustainable Development".* India Environmental Society, New Delhi, 1995.
6. D. Narasimha Reddy: "*Sustainable Development*". Edutracks. 2002. pp.35-37.
7. Exemmal: *"Construction of Certain Models for Teaching Botany using Environmental and Ethnic Resources and Testing the Efficacy of Such Models. Ph.D thesis.* University of Kerala, 1980.
8. Essential Learnings in Environmental Education: *"A Hand Book of Environmental Concepts"*, brought out by Centre for Environmental Education, Ahamedabad, 1991.
9. Glenn, J.L: *"Environmental-based Education: Creating High Performance Schools and Students".* Washington, DC: The National Environmental Education and Training *Foundation.* 2000.
10. Gopal Chandra. Pradhan: "*Environmental Awareness Among Teacher Trainees*". University News.1995.pp.10-16.
11. Kukreti, B.R.: *"Environmental Education: A Blue Print".* University News, 31(43), 1993, pp.11-14.
12. Ministry of Human Resource Development: *"Environmental Education in National Policy Documents".* 1992.
13. Maryam Larijani and Yeshodhara k: *"Relationship between Environmental Attitude* and *Environmental Awareness Among Higher Primary School Teachers of India and Iran".* Journal of all India Association for Educational Research Vol. 18. No. 3 & 4 Sept. & December 2006.
14. Marlow Ediger: *"Environmental education, teacher and the Student".* Experiments in Education. 2007. pp.17-19.
15. NCERT: *"Curriculum Frame work for Teacher Education".* New Delhi, National Council of Educational Research and Training, 2004.
16. NCERT: *"National Consultations on Environmental Education in Schools".* New Delhi, National Council of Educational Research and Training, 2000.

17. Patel, D.G. Patel, N.: *"An Investigation into the Environmental Awareness and its Enhancement in the Secondary School Teachers, Progress of Education".* 766(12), 1995, pp. 256-257.

18. Pradhan, G.C: *"Environmental Awareness among the Secondary School Teachers".* Experiments in Education, 2002, pp. 03-05.

19. Rusky, A., Wilke, R., & Beasly: *"T. A Survey of the Status of State-Level Environmental Education in the United States"*-1998 update. Journal of Environmental Education, 2001.

20. Sharma, R.C and Merle, C Tan: *"Source Book in Environmental Education for Secondary School Teachers".* UNESCO, Bangkok, 1992.

21. Santhosh Kumar Rout, Sukirti Agarwal: *"Environmental Awareness and Environmental Attitude of Students at High School Level".* Edutracks. 2006, vol. 6 (1), pp.25-26.

22. Shivakumar, K., Mangala, S.Patil: *"Influence of Environmental Education on Environmental Attitude of the Postgraduate Students".* Edutracks. 2007. Vol. 6 (8), pp.34-36.

23. Sharma, R.C: *"Implications of Environmental Education in Teacher Education".* Journal of Indian Education. 2004, pp.5-13.

24. Wheeler, K: *"The genesis of Environmental Education",* An Insights into Environmental Education, ed. G.C. Martin and K.Wheeler (Edinburgh: Oliver and Boyd, 1975, pp. 4.

25. William, E. Marden: *"Environmental Education, Historical Roots, Comparative, Perspective and Current Issues in Britain and United States"* , Vol-13, pp.6-29.

2

Review of Related Literature

In the previous chapter, Back ground of the study, Genesis of the problem, Need and Importance of the study, Statement of the problem, Objectives of the study, Education and Environment, Scope of the study are presented. In this chapter a brief review of studies related to Environmental awareness, Attitude and knowledge are presented in this second section.

The review of related literature is an important part of the scientific approach and is carried out in all areas of scientific research. This provides the research the means of getting to the frontier in his particular field of knowledge. It helps to understand the theory in the field and gives knowledge with regard to the procedures and instruments which have proved useful. It avoids un intentional replication of previous studies and keeps the researcher in a better position to interpret the significance of his own results. Thus, it could be seen that the review of related literature is very important and essential step in designing any research work.

In this chapter, review of studies conducted in this area are discussed and presented.

Reviews Related to Environmental Awareness, Attitude and Knowledge

Very few studies were carried out to know the level of environmental awareness, attitude and knowledge among the secondary school students both in India and abroad. A brief discussion of the studies conducted on primary school, secondary school and college students are discussed in the following section.

Sahaya R Mary (2005) attempted to investigate the relationship between Environmental awareness of the secondary school students with the following objectives:

(1) To study the environmental awareness among the high school students in Pondichery region.

(2) To study the relationship between the environmental awareness of the students in terms of (a) gender, (b) locality of the schools, (c) medium of instruction, (d) type of family and (e) size of the family.

(3) To study the difficulties in the environment of the students in terms of (a) caste (b) type of school and (c) religion.

The sample of the study consisted of 198 students from 10 schools in Pondichery region. The tool used in the study was Environmental opinionnaire which was prepared by the investigator. The statistical techniques used for data analysis were "t"-test and analysis of variance.

The findings of the investigation were as follows:

(*i*) Environmental awareness among the high school students is above average.

(*ii*) The medium of instruction in the school and locality of the school influence the environmental awareness among the students.

(*iii*) The type of schools and different types of religion do not affect the awareness among the students. (14:33-35)

Sreekumari, K. E. Ajitha Nayar (1998) conducted the study to know the Environmental awareness of secondary school children of Kerala. The following are the objectives of the study:

(*i*) To compare the Environmental awareness of secondary school students with respect to the following variables; a) locale b) type of institution c) difference in syllabus

(*ii*) To compare the Environmental awareness scores of government and private secondary school students based on locale.

(*iii*) To compare the environmental awareness scores of rural and urban secondary school students with respect to the proximity to polluted areas.

(*iv*) To compare the environmental awareness scores of secondary school students with respect to the educational status of parents.

The sample of the study consisted of 600 secondary school students selected on the basis of stratified random sampling technique. The tools used were: (a) A general data sheet to collect the information related to family background and educational status of parents. (b) An awareness test constructed by the researcher was used to identify the levels of Environmental awareness.

The important conclusions of the study were as follows;

(*i*) The environmental awareness of students varies with their locality, proximity to polluted areas, syllabus and type of institution.

(*ii*) The development of environmental awareness is related to the cognitive and affective domain.

(*iii*) Individual and group activities are necessary to develop higher levels of environmental awareness.

(*iv*) Syllabus has a major role in influencing the environmental awareness.(15:41-46)

Arjuna, N.K (1996) investigated the environmental attitude among rural and urban students.

The objectives of the study were:

(*i*) To study the environmental attitude of rural and urban children in high schools of Kerala.

(*ii*) To understand the components of environment in which children from rural and urban ares are not aware.

(*iii*) To know the areas in which the students from both rural and urban streams are well acquainted.

The sample of 104 ninth grade students (48 urban and 56 rural) were selected from two high schools of Trivandrum district. The tools used in the study were as follows;

(*i*) Environmental attitude scale (EAS) by Arjuna et al

(*ii*) A standardized Environmental awareness test (EAS) developed by the investigator.

The findings of the study were:

(*a*) The urban subjects possess a better attitude towards environment than the rural subjects.

(*b*) The urban subjects had better environmental awareness and attitude in the areas like, sanitation, quality of drinking water, noise pollution, and population explosion and energy conservation than the rural students.

(*c*) The rural subjects had better environmental awareness and environmental attitude on aspects like, deforestation, water resources, soil erosion, ecological adaptations and ecological cycles.

(*d*) The rural and urban subjects had better environmental awareness and attitude on ares like tropic relations, energy crises, biosphere reserves, fossil fuels and ecological pyramids.(1:20-22)

Santhosh Kumar Rout, Sukirti Agarwal (2006) attempted to discover the Environmental Awareness and Environmental Attitude of students of high school levels belonging to science and non-science stream, rural and urban backgrounds with gender differences.

Objectives of the study were:

(*i*) To determine the differences between the students of high school levels belonging to science and non – science stream.

(*ii*) To determine the difference between the students belonging to urban and rural backgrounds of high school levels in terms of their environmental awareness and environmental attitude.

(*iii*) To determine the sex difference in the students of high school level in terms of their environmental awareness and environmental attitude.

The sample of the study consisted of 96 students of (boys and girls) of class X and Intermediate colleges of Moradabad city. To measure the environmental awareness and environmental attitude of students the researcher has used the self developed tools.

The findings of the study were:

(*i*) Students of science stream have better environmental awareness and environmental attitude than the students of non-science stream.

(*ii*) The students of urban backgrounds are comparatively better in terms of their environmental awareness and environmental attitude than the students of rural background.

(*iii*) The male and female students do not differ significantly in terms of their environmental awareness and environmental attitude.(12:25-26)

Sandhya Gihar (2006) has studied the environmental responsibility among students in relation to their sex (male and female), locality (rural and urban) and subject stream (science/arts/commerce). The following were the objectives of the study;

To study the level of responsibility, with regard to a) Pollution and environmental protection among the students of IX and XII classes in respect of sex. b) Pollution and environmental protection among the students of IX and XII classes in respect of their locality c) Pollution and environmental protection among the students of IX and XII classes in respect of their subject streams.

The sample of the study comprised of 154 male and, 146 female, 100 rural, 210 urban, 143 science, 79 arts, and 78 commerce (total 300) secondary level students in Bareilly district of Uttar Pradesh. For the selection of the sample, multistage stratified random sampling technique was adopted. The tools used in the study were;

(*a*) Environmental Responsibility Assessment Inventory (ERAI). The tool was developed and standardized by Gihar, Kukreti and Shah (2002). The statistical techniques used for data analysis were, Mean, Standard Deviation and 't'-test techniques.

The findings of the investigation were;

(*i*) Male students were having higher environmental responsible behaviour than the female students.

(*ii*) The students of science background were having higher environmental responsible behaviour than their counterparts.(13:27-32)

Mercy Abraham (2005) undertook a study of Environmental Interest of Secondary School students in relation to their Environmental Attitude. Four hypotheses were proposed as follows:

(*i*) Majority of the secondary school students do not have high level of environmental interest.

(*ii*) There is a significant difference between boys and girls in their environmental interest.

(*iii*) There is a significant difference between rural and urban students in their environmental interest.

(*iv*) There will be significant correlation between environmental interest and environmental attitude of secondary school students.

The sample of the study comprised of 624 secondary school students of Kerala, selected on the basis of stratified random sampling technique. The sample consisted of 306 boys and 318 girls, the rural and urban representation being 339 and 285 respectively. The tools used were Environmental Attitude Scale (EAS) developed and standardized by the investigator. Environmental Interest Inventory (EII) developed and standardized by the investigator. The statistical techniques used for data analysis were 't'-test and Product Moment Correlation.

The findings of the investigation were:

(*i*) Only a small proportion of the secondary school students have levels of interest in environmental matters.

(*ii*) A gender difference was noticed with respect to environmental interest of secondary school students, boys are more interested in environmental matters compared to girls.

(*iii*) A locale (rural and urban) difference was also noticed with respect to the environmental interest of secondary school students; urban subjects having more interest in environmental matters compared to their rural counterparts.

(*iv*) Their existed high, positive and significant correlation between environmental interest and environmental attitude of the total sample as well as the sub samples based on gender and locale.(8:100-105)

Ifegbesan Ayodeji (2002) conducted a study to find out the views of students on environmental education elements in the junior secondary school curricula in Nigerian schools. The hypotheses tested were:

(*i*) There is no significant difference in the male and female students perception of environmental education in junior secondary school curricula.

(*ii*) There is no significant difference in the JSS II and JSS III students perception of environmental education in junior secondary school curricula.

The sample for the study comprised three hundred junior secondary school students drawn from ten secondary school in Ogun state of Nigeria. Stratified random sampling method was used for the selection of the sample. The tool used was, a questionnaire tagged Environmental Education Awareness and Attitude Questionnaire (EEAAQ) developed by the researcher. The statistical techniques used for the data analysis were Frequency counts, Percentages, Mean, Standard Deviations and 't'-tests.

The findings of the investigation were:

(*i*) Students were not adequately aware of Environmental education elements in the junior secondary schools curricula.

(*ii*) No significant difference was found between the male and female students perceptions of environmental education elements in the curriculum. (5:59-64)

Shivakumar (2007) undertook a study with the aim of studying the level of favourable attitude of the students towards environment in relation to their Environmental Education. The hypotheses tested were as follows:

(*i*) The environmental education students have higher level of favourable attitude towards environmental pollution than the non-environmental education students.

(*ii*) The sex of the students influences environmental pollution attitude of the students.

The sample for the present study comprised 120 students studying Post-Graduation Departments of Karnatak University, Dharwad. The experimental group comprised of 60 students studying in environmental course in their respective departments. The tools used were:

(*a*) Environmental Pollution Attitude Scale-developed by Dr. M.Raja Manickam. b) Personal data sheet prepared by the researcher to collect the information. The statistical techniques used for the data analysis were, Mean, Standard Deviations and 't'-test.

The findings of the investigation were:

(*i*) Standard environmental education course influences the attitude level of the students towards an environmental pollution and related issues.

(*ii*) There is no significant difference between male and female students in their attitude towards environmental pollution and related issues.

(*iii*) A standard environmental awareness education can be implemented at every level of the course irrespective of the discipline.

(*iv*) Environmental education can be the best tool for the control of environmental pollution.(16:34-36)

Ayishabi, T.C (1999) studied the environmental literature of science and non-science students at Degree level. The following were the objectives of the study:

(*a*) To find out the difference in environmental literacy and the three components of environment, viz. awareness of environment, attitude of environment and reaction towards environmental issues between science and non-science students at degree level.

(*b*) To find out the difference in environmental literacy and the three components of environment, viz. awareness of environment, attitude of environment and reaction towards environmental issues between the students of different subjects under science group and non-science groups.

The sample consisted of 200 science and 200 non-science students comprising a total of 400 final year degree students. The sample was selected from four colleges affiliated to the University of Calicut. The tools used were Environmental Literacy Inventory (Ayiashabi and Narayan Kutty). The statistical techniques used for data analysis was test of significance of difference in Means between the comparable groups.

The findings of the investigation were;

(*i*) Science students are better than the non-science students in their literacy.

(*ii*) All the science students are similar in their literacy, but among the non science students, i.e, history students are the least environmentally literate.

(*iii*) English students have better awareness of environment compared to the commerce students.(2:23-29)

Rajasrhi Roy (2006) studied the Attitude of the undergraduate pharmacy students towards environmental awareness with the following objectives,

To study the attitude and feelings of students towards the environment who are pursuing pharmaceutical degree programme in pharmaceutical science discipline. The sample of the study consisted of eighty undergraduate students studying pharmacy in three pharmacy colleges in eastern regional states. The tool used for the study was 'Environmental Consciousness Scale' which was developed by the researcher. The statistical techniques used for data analysis were Mean, Standard Deviation and't'-test.

The findings of the study were as follows:

(*i*) There is a need for including components for Environmental Awareness in curriculum.

(*ii*) There is a need for emphasizing environmental pollution monitors and control in B, Pharma courses.(11:87-93)

Shobeiri (2007) made a detailed study on Environmental awareness among secondary school students in Iran and India in relation to their residential background, sex, and type of school. The hypotheses tested were:

(*i*) There will be no significant difference in the level of environmental awareness among secondary school students in Tehran and Mysore.

(*ii*) There will be no significant difference between boys and girls students in their level of environmental awareness in Tehran and Mysore.

(*iii*) There will be no significant difference between students studying in different types of secondary schools in their level of environmental awareness in Tehara and Mysore.

The sample of the study consisted of 991 secondary school students (476 boys and 515 girls) was selected from different secondary schools in India (Mysore) and Iran (Tehran city). The students were selected from government and private school by stratified random sampling technique. The tool used in the study was, Environmental Awareness Ability Measure (EAAM) developed by Praveen Kumar Jha (1998).

The statistical techniques used for data analysis was Two-way Analysis of Variance.

The findings of the study were as follows:

(*i*) There is a significant difference in the level of students environmental awareness between two countries.

(*ii*) There is no significant difference between boys and girls students with their level of environmental awareness.

(*iii*) There is an influence of type of school management on level of students environmental awareness.

(*iv*) Type of school management has an impact on Environmental awareness of students in both the countries. In all the sub factors of students Environmental awareness, Iranian government school students scored significantly higher than their counter parts in India.(17:28-34)

Murat Gokdere (2005) conducted a study on Environmental knowledge level of primary school students in Tukey. The purpose of the study was to determine environmental knowledge level of primary school students in Turkey and it was planned to help develop a base line database that would allow effective planning of Environmental education for primary education in Turkey. A case study approach was used, and data was gathered by survey method. The sample consisted of 524 sixth, seventh and eight-grade students in six schools in the city centre, town and village of Trabzon.

The important conclusions of the study were:

(*i*) Environmental factor affect children's Environmental knowledge.

(*ii*) If children are provided with richer environment and learning material in their live, it would enhance children's Environmental knowledge.(9)

Makki, M. H (2003) conducted a study on Lebanese secondary school students Environmental Knowledge and Attitudes with the following objectives.

(*a*) To asses Lebanese secondary school students environmental knowledge and attitudes.

(*b*) To explore the relationship between participants knowledge and attitudes, biographical and academic variables, and commitment to environmentally friendly behaviour.

The sample consisted of 660 secondary school students of 10th and 11th grades. A questionnaire was administered to assess the environmental knowledge, attitudes, beliefs, intentions and commitment to environmentally friendly behaviours.

Results showed that participants had favorable attitude towards the environment but lacked in their environmental knowledge. Environmental knowledge was significantly related to parental education level, and to participants' environmental attitude, beliefs, affect, and behavioral commitments. These correlations, however, were low (r=0.17 to 0.33) indicating a definite but rather small relationship between these variables. By comparison, participants' scores on the behavior subscale were significantly and substantially correlated with their environmental affect (r=0.45) and intentions (r=0.46) suggesting that environmental intentions and affect might serve as good predictors of commitment to environmental friendly behavior. (7:21-33)

Jennifer Campbell Bradley (1999) conducted a study to assess the high school students Environmental Knowledge and Attitudes. A questionnaire was administered before and after exposure to 10 day environmental science course. Results indicated significant differences in both knowledge gain and attitudes of students after exposure. Students' environmental knowledge scores increased by 22% after they completed the environmental science course. In addition, students environmental attitudes became more environmental-ly favorable.

A statistically significant correlation was found between pre-test knowl-edge scores and pre-test attitude scores and between pos-test knowledge scores and post-test attitude scores. In both cases, students having higher knowledge scores had more favorable environmental attitudes compared with students with lower knowledge scores. (6)

S. Paraskevopoulos (1998) conducted a study on Environmental Knowledge of Elementary School Students in Greece. The education system in Greece has responded promptly to the need for environmental education (EE). However, the existing lack of relevant research may limit the functionality of EE programs in Greece. This study was conducted to develop a baseline database that would allow effective planning of EE. Specifically, the study was conducted to provide information on the environmental knowledge of 5th and 6th graders in a Greek city. A total of 686 students were surveyed.

The results indicated that children's knowledge about the environment is influenced by their immediate experience as well as by the content of their textbooks. Conclusions were (a) if people are aware of the need for and ways of protecting the environment they will act to preserve it, (b) schools should assume responsibility for educating about environmental protection, and (c) environmental edu-cation (EE) can be effective as a part of a school curriculum.(10)

Hans Kuhlemeier (1999) conducted a study on Environmental Knowledge, Attitudes and Behavior in Dutch Secondary education. In the Dutch National Assessment Program, environmental knowledge, environmental attitudes, and environmentally responsible behavior were studied in a nation wide sample of more than 9,000 students (aged ± 15 years) from 206 secondary schools. Fifty-seven percent of the 9th - grade students had a (very) positive attitude towards the environment, and 35% were prepared to take extra pains or to make (financial) sacrifices for the environment.

The students knowledge about environ-mental problems was fragmentary and often incorrect, however. Similarly, the envi-ronmentally responsible behavior of many of the students was inadequate. The rela-tion between environmental knowledge and environmental attitudes and behavior proved to be very weak. There was a substantial relation between environmental attitude, willingness to make personal sacrifices, and environmentally responsible behavior. Consistent with theories on attitudes, environmentally responsible behav-ior was more strongly connected with willingness to make sacrifices than with atti-tude towards the environment. (4)

Elvan Alp (2006) conducted a study on Children's Environmental Knowledge and Attitudes in Turkey. The aim of this study was three-fold: (1) to determine 6th , 8th and 10th grade students environmental knowledge and attitudes in Turkey; (2) to investigate the effect of the grade level and gender on students environmental knowledge and attitudes; (3) to explore how environmentally responsible behaviour is related to environmental knowledge, affects, behavioural intentions and demographic variables.

Data were obtained by the administration of the Turkish version of Children's Environmental Attitude and Knowledge Scale to 1977 students from 22 randomly selected schools located in urban areas. The data were analysed using one-way analyses of variance, independent samples 't'-test, and multiple regression analysis. A statistically significant effect of grade level was found on environmental knowledge and attitudes. While the effect of gender on attitudes towards the environment was statistically significant in favour of females, the gender difference on environmental knowledge was not statistically significant. Multiple regression analysis revealed that environmentally responsible behaviour can be predicted by behavioural intentions, environmental affects, gender, and age. Environmental knowledge appeared to be influential on behaviours not directly, but mediated by behavioural intentions and environmental affects. (3:210–223)

Tan Geok-Chin Ivy (1998) conducted a study to gather baseline data on the level of environmental knowledge, attitudes and behaviour of secondary and junior college students in Singapore. For this purpose, an instrument of 55 items was designed and tested on a sample of 1256 secondary (Grade 9) and junior college (Grade 11) students. The students mean environmental knowledge score was 70.9%. The mean correct response rates for the environmental fact, concept and generalisation subtests were 68.0%, 68.8% and 78.0% respectively. The mean environmental attitude and behaviour scores were 66.0% and 70.5% respectively.

When investigating the students main source of environmental information, it was found that the students gained most of their environmental knowledge from out-of-school sources rather than from general education at school. The majority of the students (53.7%) indicated that they gathered most of their environmental information from the print media (newspapers and magazines) and electronic media (radio and television). Only 30.7% of the students indicated that general education at school was their main source of environmental information. (18: 181-195.)

REFERENCES

1. Arjuna, N.K et al: *"Environmental Attitude Among Rural and Urban Students"*. International Educator, 11:1 & 2, 1996, pp.20-22.
2. Ayiashabi,T.C: *"Environmental Literacy of Science and Non-Science Students at Degree Level"*. Journal of All India Association for Educational Research.vol.II, No, 1&2, March 1999. pp.23-39.
3. Elvan Alp et al: *"A Statistical Analysis of Children's Environmental Knowledge and Attitudes in Turkey"*. International Research in Geographical and Environmental Education. Vol.15. No,3.2006. pp.210–223.
4. Hans Kuhlemeier, Huub Van Den Bergh, Nijs Lagerweij: *"Environmental Knowledge, Attitudes and Behavior in Dutch Secondary Education"*. Journal of Environmental Education, Vol. 30, 1999.
5. Ifegbesan Ayodeji: *"Student's Perceptions of Environmental Education Elements in Nigerian Junior Secondary School Curriculum"*. Perspectives in Education, Vol.18. No.1. pp. 59-64.

6. Jennifer Campbell Bradley, T. M. Waliczek, and J. M. Zajicek: *"Relationship between Environmental Knowledge and Environmental Attitude of High School Students".* Journal of Environmental Education, Vol. 30, 1999
7. Makki M.H, Abd-El-Khalick, F, Boujaoudes: *" Lebanese Secondary School Students' Environmental Knowledge and Attitudes".* Environmental Education Research, Vol. 9, No. 1, January 2003. pp. 21-33.
8. Mercy Abraham and N.K. Arjunan: *"Environmental Interest of Secondary School Students in Relation to their Environmental Attitude".* Perspectives in Education, Vol. 21, No. 2, 2005. pp.100-105.
9. Murat Gokdere: *"A Study on Environmental Knowledge Level of Primary Students in Turkey".* Asia–Pacific Forum on Science Learning and Teaching". Vol. 6, Issue 2, Article 5, December 2005.
10. Paraskevopoulos,S. Zafiropoulos: "Environmental Knowledge of Elementary School Students in Greece". *Journal of Environmental Education, Vol. 29, 1998.*
11. Rajasrhi Roy, et al: *"Attitude of the Undergraduate Pharmacy Students Towards Environmental Awareness".* Journal of All India Association for Educational Research, Vol. 18, No. 3&4, September 2006, pp.87-93.
12. Santhosh Kumar Rout, Sukirti Agarwal: *"Environmental Awareness and Environmental Attitude of Students at High School Level".* Edutracks, September, 2006, Vol. 6, No. 1, pp. 25-26.
13. Sandhya Gihar: *"Environmental Responsibility among Students".* Edutracks, Vol. 6, No. 1, September 2006, pp.27-32.
14. Sahaya Mary, I Paul Raj: *"Environmental Awareness among High School Students".* Edutracks. December 2005, pp. 33-35.
15. Sreekumari, K.E ands Ajitha,K: *"Environmental Awareness of Secondary School Children of Kerala".* International Educator, 13:1 & 2, 1998, pp.41-46.
16. Shivakumar, K. Mangala, S. Patil: *"Influence of Environmental Education on Environmental Attitude of the Post-Graduate Students",* Edutracks, Vol. 6, No. 8, April 2007, pp. 34-36.
17. Shobeiri, S.M., Omiidvar, B. and Prahallada, N.N: *"A Comparative Study of Environmental Awareness Among Secondary School Students in Iran and India"* International Journal of Environmental Research, Vol.1, No.1, 2007, pp.28-34.
18. Tan Geok-Chin Ivy et al: *"A Survey of Environmental Knowledge, Attitudes and Behaviour of Students in Singapore".* International Research in Geographical and Environmental Education, Vol. 7, No. 3, 1998. pp.181-195.

3

Methodology of the Study

In the previous chapter, a review of related literature and studies on various aspects of Environment, Environmental awareness, Environmental attitude and Environmental knowledge has been presented. This chapter represents the methodology adopted by the researcher in the present study. It includes the statement of the problem, selection of the variables, discussion and definitions of variables and terms, hypotheses formulated description of tools used for collection of data, sampling, administration and scoring of the tests and statistical techniques used for analysis of the data.

Statement of the Problem

The problem of the present study is *"An Investigation into the Environmental Awareness, Attitude and Knowledge among the Secondary School Students of Davangere District"*.

Selection of the Variables

A variable is a factor which is measured, manipulated and observed by the investigator (20). The variables involved in the present study are:

1. Independent variable
2. Dependent variable

Independent Variable

An Independent variable is a factor, which is measured, manipulated, observed and selected by the investigator for the purpose of determining its relationship to an observed phenomenon. (19)

The independent variables considered by the investigator in the present study are;

1. Sex / Gender——— Boys and Girls
2. Locality————— Rural / Urban
3. Types of Schools—— Government / Private

Dependent Variable

A dependent variable is the one which is measured and observed by the investigator to determine the effect of independent variable on it. (19) The dependent variables considered by the investigator in the present study are:

1. Environmental Awareness
2. Environmental Attitude
3. Environmental Knowledge

Discussions and Definitions of Variables and Terms

(1) Environment

The term Environment is defined as surrounding conditions, forces or factors potentially capable of influencing, modifying or interacting with an organism, material or other entity.

Mohua Guha in his study on Environmental education, a path way for sustainable development has defined- "Environment as the sum total of all conditions and influences that affect the development and life of organisms". (16)

Environment is interwoven in a day to day life of human beings and as such man plays a great role in preserving and improving the environment for the sake of development and better future. (21)

Benny Joseph in his book on Environment defined Environment as physical and biotic habitat that surrounds us, and is affected by all our activities to varying degrees.

(2) Environmental Education

The term environmental education is defined as way of understanding environment, and humans are part of and influence environments.

According to the International Union for the conservation of Nature and Natural Resources. "Environmental education is the process of recognizing value and clarifying concepts in order to develop skills and attitudes necessary to understand and appreciate the inter-relations among man, his culture and his biophysical surroundings". Environmental education is also entails practice in decision making and self formulating of a code of behavior about issues concerning environmental quality. (3)

Ross defines environmental education as an external force which influences the humans. Hence environmental education is an action process related to the work of almost all subject areas. It is concerned with the dynamic relationships between man and nature. It aims at improving the environmental quality. (7)

(3) Environmental Awareness

The term environmental awareness is very important in helping the social groups and individuals so as to get awareness and sensitivity to the total environment and its allied problems. (2)

Joe E, Heimlich in his studies on Environment defined Environmental awareness as the process of becoming aware of objects, qualities or relation via the senses involves the perception, processing and interpretation of impressions. (13:1-5)

(4) Environmental Attitude

The term Environmental attitude plays a vital role in helping social groups and individuals to achieve a set of values and feelings of concern for the environment and their motivation for actively participating in environmental improvement and protection.(1)

Harper in his studies on Environment and society defined environmental attitude as perceptions or values about given environmental issues. Environmental issues include the relationship between environment and society, effects of economic growth, and technology on the environment, Environmental degradation, air and water pollution, green house effect, global warming and numerous other environmental problems. (12)

(5) Environmental Knowledge

The knowledge of environment also plays vital role in helping the social groups and individuals so as to gain variety of expressions and get a basic understanding of the environment and its associated problems.

Desinger in his studies defined Environmental Knowledge is that, where we take in and understand information about an environment and then make decisions, form judgments, take opinions or make a forecast about environment. This is generally done by using rules about the world that we have worked out through having lots of information about environment from the past, data leads to information and information leads to knowledge about environment.(4)

(6) Gender

Gender refers to Sex of the Sample. Boys and Girls are selected to represent different gender. In the present study the secondary school 9th standard boys and girls were selected as the sample.

(7) Types of Schools

Types of schools refer to two types of schools existing in our secondary education system i.e. government and private schools are selected.

(*a*) Government Secondary Schools: These are the secondary Schools run by the state government

(*b*) Private Secondary Schools: These are the schools run by management and the private bodies.

(8) Locality:

Refers to background of the students, Rural and Urban background.

(*a*) *Rural:* These are the areas where the population is found below 50,000

(*b*) *Urban:* These are the areas where population is found above 50,000

Hypotheses

Based upon the discussions of variables and also keeping in view the objectives of the study, the following research hypotheses have been formulated.

1. There is no significant difference in the environmental awareness among the secondary school Boys and Girls.
2. There is no significant difference in the environmental awareness among the Rural and Urban Secondary school students.

   Sub Hypotheses

   2.1. There is no significant difference in the environmental awareness among the Rural and Urban secondary school Boys.

   2.2. There is no significant difference in the environmental awareness among the Rural and Urban secondary school Girls.
3. There is no significant difference in the environmental awareness among the students of Govt, and Private Secondary schools.

   Sub Hypotheses

   3.1. There is no significant difference in the environmental awareness among the Boys of Govt, and Private Secondary schools.

3.2. There is no significant difference in the environmental awareness among the Girl students of Govt, and Private Secondary schools.

4. There is no significant difference in the environmental attitude among the secondary school Boys and Girls.

5. There is no significant difference in the environmental attitude among the Rural and Urban Secondary school students.

Sub Hypotheses

5.1. There is no significant difference in the environmental attitude among the Rural and Urban secondary school Boys students.

5.2. There is no significant difference in the environmental attitude among the Rural and Urban secondary school Girls.

6. There is no significant difference in the environmental attitude among the Students of Government and Private Secondary schools.

Sub Hypotheses

6.1. There is no significant difference in the environmental attitude among the Boys of Govt, and Private Secondary schools.

6.2. There is no significant difference in the environmental attitude among the Girl students of Govt, and Private Secondary schools.

7. There is no significant difference in the environmental knowledge among the secondary school Boys and Girls.

8. There is no significant difference in the environmental knowledge among the Rural and Urban Secondary school students.

Sub Hypotheses

8.1. There is no significant difference in the environmental knowledge among the Rural and Urban secondary school Boys.

8.2. There is no significant difference in the environmental knowledge among the Rural and Urban secondary school Girls.

9. There is no significant difference in the environmental knowledge among the Students of Government and Private Secondary schools.

Sub Hypotheses

9.1. There is no significant difference in the environmental knowledge among the Boys of Government and Private Secondary schools.

9.2. There is no significant difference in the environmental knowledge among the Girl students of Government and Private Secondary schools.

10. There is no significance interaction effect of sex and locality on environmental awareness.
11. There is no significance interaction effect of sex and types of secondary schools on environmental awareness.
12. There is no significance interaction effect of types of schools and locality on environmental awareness
13. There is no significance interaction effect of sex and locality on environmental attitude.
14. There is no significance interaction effect of sex and types of secondary schools on environmental attitude.
15. There is no significance interaction effect of types of schools and locality on environmental attitude.
16. There is no significance interaction effect of sex and locality on environmental knowledge.
17. There is no significance interaction effect of sex and types of secondary schools on environmental knowledge.
18. There is no significance interaction effect of types of schools and locality on environmental knowledge.

Descreptions of the Tools Used for The Collection of The Data

Based on the review of related literature and personal experience and also keeping in view the variables and the objectives of the study the, investigator has used the following tools for the collection of relevant data.

1. Environmental Awareness Ability Measure (Praveen Kumar Jha, 1998). (17)
2. Taj Environmental Attitude Scale (Haseen Taj, 2001) (11)
3. Environmental Knowledge Test constructed by the researcher was used to investigate the Environmental Knowledge among the secondary school students.

(See appendix A-D for the tools used by the researcher)

Environmental Awareness Ability Measure (EAAM)

The tool was constructed and standardized by Praveen Kumar Jha, 1998. The tool is meant for assessing the Environmental Awareness of students of age group 13-16 years studying in 9th, 10th, 11th and 12th classes. The test consists of 51 items in the different areas like, causes of pollution, conservation of forest, air, energy conservation, conservation of human health, conservation of wild-life and animal husbandry.

The test was standardized on 300 Boys and 300 Girls. Adequate care has been taken by the constructor to make the sample a true representative of population.

Scoring: There are 51 items in Environmental Awareness Ability Measure scale. Each agreed item carries the value of one mark and each disagree item of zero mark but the negative items are scored inversely. Thus, on the total scale the scores ranged between 0-51. The scale gives a composite score of environmental awareness ability of the subject.

The reliability and validity of the test were obtained by using different methods and were conformed by each other.

Reliability coefficients of the test have been determined by Split-half method, K-R method and thirdly by test–retest method. The reliability coefficient was found to be 0.61 in Split-half method and 0.84 in K-R method and in the Test retest method with an interval of 3 and 6 months it was found to be 0.74 and 0.71 respectively.

Besides being good reliability the test is valid too. The Validity coefficients of the test have been found by comparing the present scale with the Environmental awareness scale developed by Tarniji and the coefficients of correlation was found to be 0.83.Thus this test consists of adequate degree of reliability and validity, Hence it is concluded that the present test is reliable and valid.

Taj Environmental Attitude Scale (TEAS)

This tool was constructed and standardized by the Haseen Taj, 2001. This scale is meant for assessing the Environmental Attitude of Students of age group 14 to 18 + years studying in the classes 9, 10, and 11th. The scale consists of six areas like Population Explosion, Health and Hygiene, Pollutants, Wild life, Forests and Environmental concerns.

There are 61 items were present in the test and it is standardized on 600 students which includes both boys and girls and the sample consists of students from 9th,10th and 11th with their age groups ranging from 14 to 18 years.

Scoring: In the present scale each item alternative is assigned with a weightage ranging from 4(strongly Agree) to 1(strongly disagree) for favourable items. In case of unfavourable items the scoring is reversed i.e. from 1(strongly agree) to 4(strongly disagree). Hence the attitude score of an individual is the sum total of item scores on all the six areas. Hence the range of scores is from 61 to 244 with the higher score indicating the more favorable attitude towards environment and vice-versa.

The reliability and validity of the scale was estimated by using different methods. The reliability coefficients were estimated by Split-half (odd-even and 1st half -2nd half) and test-retest reliability coefficients with a time gap of one month. The reliability coefficients for test–retest method was found to be 0.77 for Split-half i.e. odd even method it was found to be 0.82 and for 1st half-2nd half method it was found to be 0.81.

Besides high reliability Taj Environmental Attitude Scale posses high content Validity. The concurrent validity of the scale was determined by administering a parallel scale developed by the researcher with the same number of items worded differently by retaining the theme.

The scale also posses cross validity as the sample used for establishing the reliability of the scale was other than one used for try- out of the scale. Hence the present scale is said to be valid for assessing the Environmental attitudes.

Construction of Environmental Knowledge Test for Secondary School Students

The following stages and steps were followed in constructing the test.

Stage-I

Step-1: Planning the test

Step-2: Preparation of the test- pooling and writing of items.

Stage-II

Step-3: Trying out the test

Step-4: Item analysis in terms of–(*i*) Difficulty Index and (*ii*) Item Validity

Stage–III

Step-5: Finalisation of items based on item analysis

Stage-IV

Step-6 Evaluation of the test in terms of (*i*) Reliability and (*ii*) Validity

The above mentioned steps are described in detail in the following pages.

Step-1: Planning the test: The construction of the test must start by a consideration of the limitations under which the test has to be developed, which includes the detailed set of specifications as to the purpose of the test. Very careful planning is required for the preparation of the test. The first and the foremost step in planning a test are to define the objectives that are to be measured by the test. If the objectives and outcomes are clear cut and readily identified, the problem would be comparatively simple.

The Environmental Knowledge of the students can be evaluated through an essay type as well as objective type questions, but the investigator has chosen objective type questions specially the multiple choice type of questions for the test. The construction of the environmental knowledge test is depending more and more on secondary school curriculum. Out line of the content is important because the content is the actual vehicle through which the objectives are to be achieved. So the test should reflect all or approximate portion of different topics.

Step-2: Preparing the test-pooling and writing of items: The test items were pooled and written by referring to text books, reference books. Multiple choice types of items were prepared as they are regarded as the most valuable items. The test consist of 100 items from four areas of environment i.e., Nature, Ecological relationship, Pollution, Health and Hygiene. (Out of these 34 items was drawn from nature, 31 are from ecological relationship, and 28 are from pollution and 7 from Health and hygiene). The items thus prepared were scrutinized by experts and senior teachers from secondary schools. In the light of the suggestions given by them, necessary modifications were made in certain items. Thus a draft consists of 100 items for the tryout. See Appendix–C for the Environmental knowledge test (Draft) with the directions and scoring key.

Step-3: Trying out the test: After the test was prepared according to plan it was ready to be given a trial in actual use. The questionnaire was scrutinized to correct the typographical errors if any. Since, it is impossible in advance to know exactly how good the test is, the tryout should be considered as one of the important necessary steps in constructing in final form.

The purpose of the experimental tryout is to obtain the data concerning the following:

1. The difficulty of the each test item.
2. The discriminating power of each test item
3. The effectiveness of each distracter for each multiple choice test item.
4. The adequacy of the directions and the test format. (9:285)

The final draft thus prepared was tried out on a sample of 400 high school students attending the 9th standard classes in various secondary schools in Davangere District, which was selected at random.

Step-4: Item Analysis: The test was administered to 400 high school students and their answer books were scored and master chart containing question wise marks and total marks was prepared. For the purpose of determining item difficulty indices and item validity, the scores were arranged in descending order. The answer paper was divided in to three groups such as high groups, average group and low group. The upper 27 percent of the answer papers forms the higher group; the lower 27 percent of the answer papers forms the lower group and the rest 46 percent in the middle were taken as the average group.

The number of answer papers in both the extreme groups is 108 each as the total number of papers were 400. The average group was kept aside and a paper of the other two groups (High and Low groups) was taken for the item analysis.

Facility Index (FI): The Facility index is defined as the percentage of the groups who answered the item correctly. The larger the value of the index is, the easier the item. The numerical value of the index of difficulty of a test item neither is nor determined solely by the content of the item. It reflects also the ability of the groups responding to the item. (6:228).

Facility Index (FI) was calculated by using the following formula:

$$FI = \frac{\text{No, right (High)} + \text{No. right (Low)}}{\text{Total no. in High} + \text{Low group}} \times 100$$

The following table indicates item difficulty indices:

Table 3.1: Facility Indices of 100 Items of Environmental Knowledge

Item number	No. of students answered correctly higher group	No. of students answered in correctly in lower group	FI = (No, right (High) + No. right (Low)) / (Total no. in High + Low group) × 100
1	2	3	4
1	74	54	79
2	67	45	70
3	74	16	55
4	03	12	09
5	72	47	73
6	10	07	10
7	11	28	24
8	79	33	69
9	68	20	54
10	71	51	75
11	80	65	90
12	81	55	84
13	00	08	05
14	76	58	82
15	70	21	56

1	2	3	4
16	68	14	51
17	77	14	56
18	68	22	56
19	77	24	62
20	14	25	24
21	09	18	17
22	73	14	54
23	29	16	28
24	38	11	30
25	75	10	52
26	07	21	35
27	66	25	56
28	10	09	12
29	70	12	51
30	69	30	61
31	72	19	56
32	70	29	61
33	11	07	11
34	80	65	90
35	74	31	65
36	76	43	73
37	78	48	78
38	78	46	77
39	72	64	84
40	77	33	68
41	38	22	37
42	11	18	18
43	79	30	67

1	2	3	4
44	79	49	79
45	77	37	70
46	74	24	60
47	16	23	24
48	75	45	74
49	67	43	68
50	69	11	49
51	15	07	14
52	10	06	10
53	58	16	46
54	65	21	53
55	03	27	19
56	74	31	65
57	25	25	31
58	79	28	66
59	00	42	26
60	81	25	65
61	3	10	08
62	78	19	60
63	09	17	16
64	75	12	54
65	17	42	36
66	78	14	57
67	09	47	35
68	66	27	57
69	07	13	12
70	57	17	46
71	19	21	25

1	2	3	4
72	42	30	44
73	46	14	36
74	44	29	45
75	72	26	60
76	08	12	12
77	68	37	65
78	49	18	41
79	71	38	67
80	63	38	62
81	19	14	20
82	71	32	64
83	65	35	62
84	74	41	71
85	50	17	41
86	57	27	52
87	71	31	63
88	76	32	67
89	78	37	71
90	35	06	25
91	64	10	46
92	75	21	59
93	15	14	18
94	80	51	81
95	02	20	14
96	73	24	60
97	71	30	62
98	77	37	70
99	73	26	61
100	68	07	46

Item Validity

The validity index of an item (i.e., its discriminative power) is determined to the extent to which the given item discriminates among examinees who differ sharply in the function (or functions) measured by the test as a whole. A number of methods have been devised for use in determining the discriminative power of an item. (8)

In the present study Johnson's Upper-Lower Index method was followed. Discriminative Index is a measure of the correlation (relationship) between the item and the total test score. Like the coefficient of correlation, the Discriminative Index ranges from 1.00 through 0 to -1.00.

The Discriminative Index (DI) was calculated by using the following formula.

$$DI = \frac{\text{No. Right. High group-No. right. Low group}}{\text{No. in EITHER High or Low group}}$$

Table 3.2 : Validities of Items of Environmental Knowledge Test (n = 400)

Item number	No. of students answered correctly in higher group	No. of students answered correctly in lower group	$DI = \frac{\text{No, right High group - No. right Low group}}{\text{No. in EITHER High or Low group}}$
1	2	3	4
1	74	54	0.24
2	67	45	0.27
3	74	16	0.71
4	03	12	0.11
5	72	47	0.30
6	10	7	0.03
7	11	28	0.20
8	79	33	0.56

1	2	3	4
09	68	20	0.59
10	71	51	0.24
11	80	65	0.18
12	81	55	0.32
13	00	8	0.98
14	76	58	0.22
15	70	21	0.60
16	68	14	‘0.66
17	77	14	0.77
18	68	22	0.56
19	77	24	0.65
20	14	25	0.13
21	09	18	0.11
22	73	14	0.72
23	29	16	0.16
24	38	11	0.33
25	75	10	0.80
26	07	21	0.17
27	66	25	0.50
28	10	09	0.01
29	70	12	0.71
30	69	30	0.48
31	72	19	0.65
32	70	29	0.50
33	11	7	0.04
34	80	65	0.18
35	74	31	0.53
36	76	43	0.40
37	78	48	0.37
38	78	46	0.39

1	2	3	4
39	72	64	0.09
40	77	33	0.54
41	38	22	0.19
42	11	18	0.08
43	79	30	0.60
44	79	49	0.37
45	77	37	0.49
46	74	24	0.61
47	16	23	0.08
48	75	45	0.37
49	67	43	0.29
50	69	11	0.71
51	15	7	0.09
52	10	6	0.04
53	58	16	0.51
54	65	21	0.54
55	03	27	0.29
56	74	31	0.53
57	25	25	0.00
58	79	28	0.62
59	00	42	0.51
60	81	25	0.69
61	03	10	0.08
62	78	19	0.72
63	09	17	0.09
64	75	12	0.77
65	17	42	0.30
66	78	14	0.79
67	09	47	0.46
68	66	27	0.48
69	07	13	0.07

1	2	3	4
70	57	17	0.49
71	19	21	0.02
72	42	30	0.14
73	46	14	0.39
74	44	29	0.18
75	72	26	0.56
76	08	12	0.04
77	68	37	0.38
78	49	18	0.38
79	71	38	0.40
80	63	38	0.30
81	19	14	0.06
82	71	32	0.48
83	65	35	0.37
84	74	41	0.40
85	50	17	0.40
86	57	27	0.37
87	71	31	0.49
88	76	32	0.54
89	78	37	0.50
90	35	6	0.35
91	64	10	0.66
92	75	21	0.66
93	15	14	0.01
94	80	51	0.35
95	02	20	0.22
96	73	24	0.60
97	71	30	0.50
98	77	37	0.49
99	73	26	0.58
100	68	07	0.75

Step-5: Finalisation of Items Based on Item Analysis: Index of item difficulty and item Validity coefficient are calculated for individual test items. As a result of these two analysis, items numbered, 1, 2, 4, 6, 7, 10, 11, 13, 14, 20, 21, 23, 26, 28, 33, 34, 41, 42, 47, 49, 51, 52, 55, 57, 59, 61, 63, 65, 67, 69, 71, 72, 74, 76, 81, 93 and 95 were deleted

The remaining 62 items carrying total 62 marks constituted the final test. It may be added here that too easy and too difficult item and items with Discriminative Index ranging from 0.30 to 0.90 and Facility Index from 40% to 90% were added. (5) Thus the final form contains 62 items. Then the test items were arranged on the basis of difficulty level in the final test.

Step-6: Evaluation of Environmental Knowledge Test: The final test was evaluated with the help of reliability and validity of the test.

Reliability of the Test

The reliability of a test is its ability to yield consistent result from one set of measure to another. It refers to the extent to which a measuring device yields consistent result upon testing and retesting. (10) The test retest reliability of the test was worked out (with a test-retest interval of 3 weeks) by administering the test on a representative sample of 100 subjects. The obtained coefficient of test-retest reliability is 0.72. Consistency reliability was calculated by Split-half method and it was found to be 0.68 (n = 200)

Validity of the Test

A test is valid one if it measures what it intends to measure or that it must measure the objective or such an aspect of objective as the test claims that it is measuring. It always refers to the purpose of the test.(14) The Intrinsic validities of the test was calculated and it ranged from 0.82(n = 200) to 0.84 (n = 100).

The reliability and validity coefficients that the test is reasonably dependable measure of Environmental Knowledge of secondary school students of Davangere district.

Reasons for selecting the above mentioned Tools for the present study

1. The tools have been prepared on secondary school going students as the sample of the study
2. The selected tools have high validity and reliability coefficients
3. The selected tools can be administered to a group of 40-50 students without any difficulty
4. The test can be easily understood by the average students
5. The system of scoring of the above tests is easy and can be done quickly
6. The tests have been specially developed to suit Indian conditions
7. The above mentioned tools were used by many investigators in their studies

Sampling

The primary purpose of research is to discover principles that have universal application. But, to study a whole population in order to arrive at a generalization would be impracticable if not impossible. Given the dynamic nature of population, it is possible that the characteristics of the population would change by the time the research in studying those population are completed. It becomes important to study such populations as they exist at the time of research and report them to the relative to a time frame. (18)

After finalizing the variables of the present study, consideration was given to whether the entire population is to be made the subject for data collection or a particular group is to be selected as representative of the whole population. The entire population here refers to all the 9th standard secondary school students of Davangere district. The selection of a group as a representative of the entire population was found to be more convenient and suitable. This technique leads to a considerable saving of time, effort and finance.

The number of students selected is small, and so it is possible to make a detailed and intensive study. This generally leads to more accurate and reliable results.

The process of sampling makes it possible to draw valid conclusions or generalizations on the basis of careful observations or manipulation of variables within a relatively small proportion of the total universe.(15) Samples are not selected haphazardly but are chosen in a deliberate way so that the influence of chance of probability can be estimated.

The purpose of the present study is to investigate the environmental awareness, attitude and knowledge of secondary school students of Davangere district. The population from which the sample for the study was drawn consisted of students studying during the year 2007-08 in 9th standard government and private secondary schools of Davangere District. The sample was selected using the stratified random sampling procedure. This procedure was preferred in order to give representation to all types of secondary schools and also to make the sample true representative of the population.

At first stage, 36 secondary schools were selected. At the second stage the numbers of 9th standard secondary school students were selected proportionately. Both at first and the second stage, the sample has been drawn randomly.

Sample

Total number of Secondary Schools selected in Davangere District:

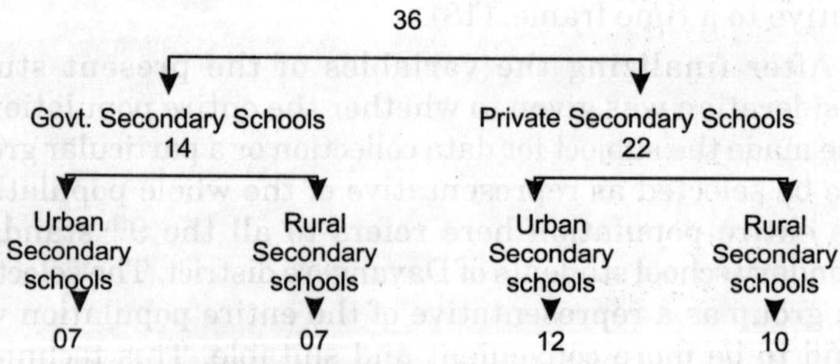

Fig. 3.1: Flow Chart of Sampling

At first stage, the secondary schools have been drawn randomly by using lots in the ratio 10:1. At the second stage random numbers have been used to select the required numbers of 9th standard students from each secondary school.

The details regarding the number of secondary school both government and private, the number of boys and girls is presented in the table to follow.

Table 3.3: Statement showing the Number of Secondary Schools–their Type, Locality and the Number of Secondary School Students drawn from each Secondary school

Sl. No.	Name of the School	Locality of the school	Type of school Govt./ Private	Number of students Selected		
				Boys	Girls	Total
1	2	3	4	5	6	7
1.	Mothi veerappa High school, Davangere	U	G	20	20	40
2.	D.R.R. High school, Davangere	U	P	20	20	40
3.	S.T.J. High school, Davangere	U	P	20	20	40
4.	S.V. High school, Davangere	U	P	20	20	40
5.	H.Siddappa High school, Kandagal	R	P	20	20	40
6.	Patel H.G.K High school, Attigere	R	G	20	20	40
7.	A.K. High school, Bada	R	P	20	20	40
8.	Govt. High school, Turchagatta	R	G	20	20	40
9.	Ex Municipal High school, Davangere	U	G	20	20	40
10.	H.Shivalingappa High school, Anaji	R	G	20	20	40
11.	M.B. High school, Davavangere	U	P	20	20	40

1	2	3	4	5	6	7
12.	M.G.M.R High School, Davangere	U	P	20	20	40
13.	Sree Rudreswara High school, Hebbal	R	P	20	20	40
14.	Govt. High school, Harihar	U	G	20	20	40
15.	Beeralingeswara High school, Malebennur	R	G	20	20	40
16.	Girijamma High school, Harihar	U	P	20	20	40
17.	M.K.E.T High school, Harihar	U	P	20	20	40
18.	M.H. High school, Holesirigere	R	P	20	20	40
19.	Govt. High school, Jagalur	U	G	20	20	40
20.	S.Maruti High school, Anaberu	R	G	20	20	40
21.	Bedara kannappa High school, Jagalur	U	P	20	20	40
22.	Tirumalashwara High school, Holebele	R	P	20	20	40
23.	Govt. High school, Honnali	U	G	20	20	40
24.	Sree Ragavendra High School, Ujjinipura	R	G	20	20	40
25.	Akkamahadevi High School, Honnali	U	P	20	20	40
26.	Sree Siddeswara High School, Nyamathi	R	P	20	20	40
27.	Govt, High School, Harapanahalli	U	G	20	20	40

1	2	3	4	5	6	7
28.	Gurudeva High School, Kammathahalli	R	G	20	20	40
29.	T.M.A.E. High School, Harapanahalli	U	P	20	20	40
30.	Sree Naradamuni High School, Chigateri	R	P	20	20	40
31.	Govt. High School, Channagiri	U	G	20	20	40
32.	Valkimi High School, Doddagutta	R	P	20	20	40
33.	Navachetana High School, Channagiri	U	P	20	20	40
34.	Mannamma High School, Channagiri	U	P	20	20	40
35.	Beralingeswara High School, Santebennur	R	P	20	20	40
36.	Madhukeswara High School, Hodigere	R	P	20	20	40

Note: U=Urban, R= Rural, P= Private school, G=Govt. school

The sample was considered to be fairly true representative of the population since it included all categories of secondary schools and the sample included both boys and girls studying in government and private, urban and rural secondary schools of Davangere district. The proportion of the sample of urban and rural secondary school students is almost in the ratio of 1:1 (770:680), boys and girls sample is also in the ratio of 1:1(720:720).

Administration and Scoring of the Tests

The researcher administered the following tools to the selected sample in order to obtain the required data. Environmental Awareness Ability Measure Scale, Taj Environmental Attitude Scale and Environmental Knowledge Test were administered to the selected students on different session from the 4th week of October to 4th week of December during the year 2007. The researcher has selected this period for administration of tests because in most of the secondary schools first semester would have been completed and the students will be at the verge of the second semester. This is done to ensure that all students are at uniform level of subject attainment. The tools requires 3 hours for the actual administration of the tests, besides the investigator had spent nearly 1hour for establishing rapport, giving instructions, distributing and collecting the booklets, etc.

Tests were administered in three sessions for 2 days in each school. Environmental awareness ability measure scale was administered in the morning session and Taj environmental attitude scale was administered in the afternoon session in one day, and in the second day Environmental knowledge test was administered in the morning session.

The administrations of the tests were done by the investigator him self. About 2-3 class teachers were present during testing. They helped the investigator to administer the tests efficiently.

The following points were kept in view while administering the tools;

1. The directions for each tool were given exactly as provided in the cover page of the booklet.
2. Seating arrangements were made as it was done for examination. (2 students were seated in each bench)
3. The researcher has taken the help of the class teachers while distributing and collecting the booklets and also to maintain discipline in the test hall. When the testing in 36 secondary schools was completed, the sample obtained was 1440.

Scoring

Scoring was done following the guidelines, scoring keys provided in the respective test manuals. After careful scoring, the raw scores were obtained in respect of each. To make the raw scores obtained from the other tests meaningful, they were subjected to various statistical tools so that the significance of various hypotheses could be tested. In the following pages, the researcher has discussed the various statistical techniques used for the analysis of the data.

Statistical Techniques used for Analysis of the Data

The researcher has used the following statistical techniques for the analysis of the data.

(*a*) Mean and Standard Deviations were calculated for the scores in the group.

(*b*) Test of Significance i.e. paired't'-test was used to compare the different groups in respect of dependent variable.

(*c*) Coefficient of correlation was calculated to establish validity and reliability of the Environmental Knowledge Test constructed by the investigator.

(*d*) Two way ANOVA was used to test the hypotheses.

In Summary, this chapter has given a detailed account of the methodology adopted by the researcher in the present study. In the next chapter, the analysis and interpretation of the data has been presented and discussed.

REFERENCES

1. Arcury, Thomas, A: *"Environmental Attitude and Knowledge"* Human Organisation. 49 (4). 1990.
2. Bhanumathi,R: *"Environmental Education Strategies and Approaches"* in Environmental Issues, New Delhi; Reliance Publishing House, 2003.
3. Balkrishna P: *"A Study on Environmental Knowledge, Environmental Attitude and Perception Regarding Environmental Education Among Preservice and In-service sSecondary School Teachers.* Thesis (Ph.D) M. S. University, Baroda, 1991
4. Desinger, J.F: *"What Research says: Environmental Education"* The Ecologist, Vol. 85, 1985, pp.10-28.

5. Edwin Harper. Erika. S. Harper: *"Preparing Objective Examinations: A Handbook for Teachers, Students and Examiners"*. Prentice Hall of India Private Limited, New Delhi, 1992.
6. Ebel, Robert L. and Frisble David A: *"Essentials of Educational Measurement"*. Fifth Edition, New Delhi: Prentice Hall of India Private Limited, 1991, pp. 228.
7. Gopalkrishnan: *"Impact of Environmental Education on Primary School Children in Avinashilingam"*. Fifth Survey of Educational Research. Vol II.
8. Garret, Henry E: *"Statistics in Psychology and Education"*. Bombay Vakils, Feffer and Simons Pvt. Ltd., 1981, pp.151-181.
9. Grounlund Norman E: *"Measurement and Evaluation in Teaching"*. Third edition, New York: Mac Millan Publishing Co., Inc., 1976, pp-285.
10. Guilford, J.P: *"Fundamental Statistics in Psychology and Education"*. Fourth edition, New York: Mc Graw Hill Book Company, 1965, pp. 368.
11. Haseen Taj: *"Manual for Taj Environmental Attitude Scale"* TEAS, Agra; Nandini Enterprises, 2001, pp. 1-13.
12. Harper, Charles L: *"Environment and Society"*: Human Perspectives on Environmental Issues, Printce Hill. New Jersey, 1996.
13. Joe E, Heimlich: *"Thesaurus of Environmental Education Terms"*. Columbus.The Ohio State University, North American Association for Environmental Education (NAAEE). 1999, pp. 1-5.
14. John W Best and James V Kahn: *"Research in Education"*. Prentice Hall of India. Pvt. Ltd., New Delhi.
15. Lokesh Koul: *"Methodology of Educational Research"*. Vikas Publishing House Pvt. Ltd. 2000.
16. Mohua Guha and Aparajita Chattopadhyay: *"Environmental Education: A Pathway for Sustainable Development"*. Environmental Issues. New Delhi. Reliance Publishing House.
17. Praveen Kumar Jha: *"Manual for Environmental Awareness Ability Measure"* (EAAM), Agra; National Psychological Corporation, 1998, pp.1-19.
18. Smith Sebasto N J: *"Potential Guide lines for Conducting and Reporting Environmental Educational Research"*. Qualitative Methods of Inquiry. Vol. II, 2000, pp. 9-26.

19. Thorndike, R: *"Personal Selection Test and Measurement Techniques"*. New York: John Wiley and Sons Inc., February, 1996, pp.245.

20. Tuckman, Bruce W: *"Conducting Educational Research"*. New York: Harcourt Brace Jovanovich Inc., 1978, pp. 58-59.

21. Vijayalakshmi,S: *"Environmental Education: Concern and strategies"* in Environmental Issues. New Delhi; Reliance Publishing House, 2003.

4

Analysis and Interpretation of Data

In the previous chapter on methodology of the study, variables, tools used for the collection of data, sampling and the statistical techniques used in the study are discussed.

In this chapter, the data collected are analysed, discussion is done and the result obtained are interpreted.

Testing of Hypotheses

The Hypotheses formulated were tested using the test of significance i.e. paired 't'–test and also by multiple classification analysis of variance (Two way ANOVA).

Hypothesis : 1

There is no significant difference in the environmental awareness among the secondary school Boys and Girls.

Table 4.1: Significance of Difference in Mean Environmental Awareness Scores between Secondary School Boys and Girls

Particulars	No. of Students	Environmental Awareness scores		Mean difference	t-value	P-value
		Mean	S D			
Boys	736	40.1	6.8	0.1	0.26	0.80 Ns
Girls	736	40.2	7.8			

Ns—Non significant.

The't'- test results in the table no, 04 shows no significant difference in mean environmental awareness scores among Boys and Girls. Therefore the hypothesis, which states that there is no significant difference in environmental awareness among the secondary school boys and Girls was accepted.

From this, it may be concluded that the girls and boys of secondary school students do not differ in their environmental awareness. The results obtained in this study are corroborated by the findings reported by Garmina Darshan (1996) and Sukirti Agaarwal (2006).

Hypothesis-2

There is no significant difference in the environmental awareness among the Rural and Urban Secondary school students.

Table 4.2: Significance of Difference in Mean Environmental Awareness Scores Between Rural and Urban Secondary School students

Characteristic	Particulars	No. of Students	Environmental Awareness scores		Mean difference	t-value	P- value
			Mean	S D			
Locality	Rural	640	38.7	6.4	2.9	7.68*	<0.01
	Urban	832	41.6	7.7			

*Significant at 0.01 level of significance.

The obtained 't' value 7.68 is significant at 0.01 level of significance as it is more than the table value 2.58. Hence, the hypothesis is rejected.

Further, when means are compared, we can conclude that environmental awareness of urban students (M = 41.6) is better than the rural students. (M = 38.7). The higher environmental awareness of urban students could be attributed to their wider social, better exposure to information via all kinds of media as well as their enhanced opportunities to experiment with nature and its components.

Sub Hypotheses:

2.1-There is no significant difference in the environmental awareness among the Rural and Urban secondary school Boys.

Table 4.3: Significance of Difference in Mean Environmental Awareness Scores between Rural and Urban Secondary School Students

Characteristic	Particulars	No. of Students	Environmental Awareness scores		Mean difference	t-value	P- value
			Mean	S D			
Boys	Rural	340	37.5	6.4	4.4	9.33*	< 0.01
	Urban	380	41.9	6.4			

*Significant at 0.01 level of significance

The obtained 't' value 9.33 is significant at 0.01 level of significance as it is more than the table value 2.58. Hence, the hypothesis is rejected.

Further, when means are compared, we can conclude that environmental awareness of urban boys (M = 41.9) is better than the rural students (M = 37.5). The higher environmental awareness of urban boys could be attributed to their wider social, better exposure to information via all kinds of media as well as their enhanced opportunities to experiment with nature and its components.

Sub Hypotheses:

There is no significant difference in the environmental awareness among the Rural and Urban secondary school Girls.

It is evident from the table no 07, the obtained 't' value 2.31 is significant at 0.05 level of significance as it is more than the table value 1.96. Hence, the hypothesis is rejected.

Further, when means are compared, we can conclude that environmental awareness of urban girls (M = 41.3) is better than the rural students (M = 40.0). The higher environmental awareness of urban girls could be attributed to their wider social, better exposure to information via all kinds of media as well as their enhanced opportunities to experiment with nature and its components.

Table 4.4 : Significance of Difference in Mean Environmental Awareness Scores between Rural and Urban Secondary School Students

Characteristic	Particulars	No. of Students	Environmental Awareness scores		Mean difference	t-value	P- value
			Mean	S D			
Girls	Rural	320	40.0	6.1	1.3	2.31*	< 0.05
	Urban	416	41.3	8.8			

*Significant at 0.05 level of significance.

The results obtained in this study are corroborated by the results obtained in the study that was conducted by Arjun, N.K. (1996) and Mercy Abraham (2005).

Hypothesis-3

There is no significant difference in the environmental awareness among the students of Govt, and Private Secondary schools.

Table 4.5 : Significance of difference in Mean Environmental Awareness Scores between Government and Private Secondary School Students

Characteristic	Particulars	No. of Students	Environmental Awareness scores		Mean difference	t-value	P- value
			Mean	S D			
Types of Schools	Govt.	576	38.6	6.4	1.8	4.65*	<0.01
	Private	888	40.4	7.8			

*Significant at 0.01 level of significance.

The data in the above table indicates that, the obtained 't' value 4.65 is significant at 0.01 level of significance as it is more than the table value 2.58. Hence, the hypothesis is rejected.

Further, when means are compared, we can conclude that environmental awareness of students of private schools

(M = 40.4) is better than the students of government schools (M = 38.6). This may be due to more opportunities given to private school students to become familiar with their environment and community centered co–curricular programmes in private schools.

Sub Hypotheses

There is no significant difference in the environmental awareness among the Boys of Govt, and Private Secondary schools.

Table 4.6 : Significance of Difference in Mean Environmental Awareness Scores between Government and Private Secondary School Students

Characteristic	Particulars	No. of Students	Environmental Awareness scores		Mean difference	t-value	P- value
			Mean	S D			
Boys	Govt.	288	38.8	6.9	2.0	4.11*	<0.01
	Private	444	40.8	6.6			

*Significant at 0.01 level of significance.

The data in the above table indicates that, the obtained 't' value 4.11 is significant at 0.01 level of significance as it is more than the table value 2.58. Hence, the hypothesis is rejected.

Further, when means are compared, we can conclude that environmental awareness of boys of private schools (M = 40.8) is better than the boys of government schools (M = 38.8). This may be due to more opportunities given to private school students to become familiar with their environment and community centered co–curricular programmes in private schools.

Sub Hypotheses

3.2-There is no significant difference in the environmental awareness among the Girl students of Govt, and Private Secondary schools.

The findings in the table no, 10 shows that, the obtained 't' value 2.61 is significant at 0.05 level of significance as it is more than the table value 1.96. Hence, the hypothesis is rejected.

Table 4.7 : Significance of Difference in Mean Environmental Awareness Scores between Government and Private Secondary School Students

Characteristic	Particulars	No. of Students	Environmental Awareness scores		Mean difference	t-value	P- value
			Mean	S D			
Girls	Govt.	288	38.5	6.0	1.6	2.61*	< 0.05
	Private	444	40.1	8.8			

*Significant at 0.05 level of significance.

Further, when means are compared, we can conclude that environmental awareness of girls of private schools (M = 40.1) is better than the girls of government schools (M = 38.5). The results obtained in this study are corroborated by the findings reported by Sreekumari, K. E (1998).

Hypothesis-4

There is no significant difference in the environmental attitude among the secondary School Boys and Girls.

Table 4.8 : Significance of Difference in Mean Environmental Attitude Scores between Secondary School Boys and Girls

Particulars	No. of Students	Environmental Attitude scores		Mean difference	t-value	P-value
		Mean	S D			
Boys	734	164.0	23.1	2.1	1.52	0.13Ns
Girls	734	166.1	30.0			

Ns-Non significant.

The't'- test results in the table no,11 shows no significant difference in mean environmental attitude scores among Boys and Girls. Therefore the hypothesis, which states that there is no significant difference in environmental attitude among the secondary school boys and girls students, was accepted.

Hypothesis-5

There is no significant difference in the environmental attitude among the Rural and Urban Secondary school students.

Table 4.9: Significance of Difference in Mean Environmental Attitude Scores between Rural and Urban Secondary School Students

Characteristic	Particulars	No. of Students	Environmental Attitude scores		Mean difference	t-value	P- value
			Mean	S D			
Locality	Rural	640	157.3	25.5	10.9	8.26*	< 0.01
	Urban	830	168.2	24.5			

*Significant at 0.01 level of significance.

The obtained 't' value 8.26 is significant at 0.01 level of significance as it is more than the table value 2.58. Hence, the hypothesis is rejected.

Further, when means are compared, we can conclude that environmental attitude of urban students (M = 168.2) is better than the rural students. (M = 157.3). The higher environmental attitude of urban students is due to their better exposure to information via all kinds of media as well as their enhanced opportunities to experiment with nature and its components. Urban environment being more polluted and congested compared to rural environment; urban subjects will be more aware of bad effects of population growth, Industrialisation, energy crises, etc. It is quite reasonable to assume that this will develop more concrete concepts about environmental aspects like biodiversity, ecological relationship, etc.

Sub Hypotheses

5.1-There is no significant difference in the environmental attitude among the Rural and Urban secondary school Boys.

Table 4.10: Significance of Difference in Mean Environmental Attitude Scores between the Boys of Rural and Urban Secondary Schools

Characteristic	Particulars	No. of Students	Environmental Attitude scores		Mean difference	t-value	P- value
			Mean	S D			
Boys	Rural	320	158.3	26.0	10.1	6.03*	< 0.01
	Urban	415	168.4	28.7			

*Significant at 0.01 level of significance.

It is evident from the table no 13, the obtained 't' value 6.03 is significant at 0.01 level of significance as it is more than the table value 2.58. Hence, the hypothesis is rejected.

Further, when means are compared, we can conclude that environmental attitude of urban boys (M = 168.4) is better than the rural boys (M = 158.3). The higher scores made by urban boys were mainly because they were made environmentally sensitive as they are often the victims of degraded natural environment, and they were better informed as they were living in a world of better media net works and also they were more concerned about ever deteriorating quality of the environment in which they were living. This difference is also due to the difference in the educational level of parents of urban and rural students and approach of the media is also the important factor.

Sub Hypotheses:

5.2-There is no significant difference in the environmental attitude among the Rural and Urban secondary school Girls.

It is evident from the table no 14, the obtained 't' value 5.73 is significant at 0.01 level of significance as it is more than the table value 2.58. Hence, the hypothesis is rejected.

Further, when means are compared, we can conclude that environmental attitude of urban girls (M = 168.0) is better than the rural girls (M = 156.4). The results obtained in this study are confirmed by the results obtained in the studies conducted by Shivakumar, K (2007) and Ayodeji (2002).

Table 4.11: Significance of Difference in Mean Environmental Attitude Scores between the Girls of Rural and Urban Secondary Schools

Characteristic	Particulars	No. of Students	Environmental Attitude scores		Mean difference	t-value	P-value
			Mean	S D			
Girls	Rural	320	156.4	25.1	11.6	5.73*	< 0.01
	Urban	415	168.0	28.7			

*Significant at 0.01 level of significance.

Hypothesis-6

There is no significant difference in the environmental attitude among the Students of Government and Private Secondary schools.

Table 4.12: Significance of Difference in Mean Environmental Attitude Scores between Government and Private Secondary School Students

Characteristic	Particulars	No. of Students	Environmental Attitude scores		Mean difference	t-value	P-value
			Mean	S D			
Types of Schools	Govt.	580	159.9	33.1	8.5	6.00*	<0.01
	Private	888	168.4	24.5			

*Significant at 0.01 level of significance.

The data in the above table indicates that the, the obtained 't' value 6.00 is significant at 0.01 level of significance as it is more than the table value 2.58. Hence, the hypothesis is rejected.

Further, when means are compared, we can conclude that environmental attitude of private school students (M = 168.4) is better than the students of government schools (M = 159.9). The findings thus revealed that private school students had developed more environmental awareness than the government school students.

Sub Hypotheses:

6.1-There is no significant difference in the environmental attitude among the Boys of Govt, and Private Secondary schools.

Table 4.13: Significance of Difference in Mean Environmental Attitude Scores between the Boys of Government and Private Secondary Schools

Characteristic	Particulars	No. of Students	Environmental Attitude scores		Mean difference	t-value	P- value
			Mean	S D			
Boys	Govt.	290	157.2	27.9	11.2	6.62*	<0.01
	Private	444	168.4	18.1			

*Significant at 0.01 level of significance.

It is evident from the table no 16, the obtained 't' value 6.62 is significant at 0.01 level of significance as it is more than the table value 2.58. Hence, the hypothesis is rejected.

Further, when means are compared, we can conclude that environmental attitude of boys of private schools (M = 168.4) is better than the boys of government schools (M = 157.2). This may be due to more opportunities given to private school students to become familiar with their environment and community centered co–curricular programmes in private schools.

Sub Hypotheses

6.2-There is no significant difference in the environmental Attitude among the Girl students of Govt, and Private Secondary schools.

The findings in the table no,17 shows that , the obtained 't' value 2.54 is significant at 0.05 level of significance as it is more than the table value 1.96. Hence, the hypothesis is rejected.

Table 4.14: Significance of Difference in Mean Environmental Attitude Scores between the Girls of Government and Private Secondary School Students

Characteristic	Particulars	No. of Students	Environmental Awareness scores		Mean difference	t-value	P- value
			Mean	S D			
Girls	Govt.	290	162.7	37.4	5.7	2.54*	<0.05
	Private	444	168.4	23.7			

*Significant at 0.05 level of significance.

Further, when means are compared, we can conclude that environmental attitude of girls of private schools (M = 168.4) is better than the girls of government schools (M = 162.7).

Hypothesis-7

There is no significant difference in the environmental knowledge among the secondary school Boys and Girls.

Table 4.15 : Significance of Difference in Mean Environmental knowledge Scores between Secondary School Boys and Girls

Particulars	No. of Students	Environmental knowledge scores		Mean difference	t-value	P-value
		Mean	S D			
Boys	739	30.5	10.3	0.5	0.79	0.43Ns
Girls	739	31.0	9.2			

Ns-Non significant at 0.05 level.

The't'-test results in the table no, 18 shows no significant difference in the mean environmental knowledge scores among boys and girls. Therefore the hypothesis which states that there is no significant difference in environmental knowledge among the secondary schools boys and girls students was accepted.

Hypothesis-8

There is no significant difference in the environmental

knowledge among the Rural and Urban Secondary school students.

Table 4.16 : Significance of Difference in Mean Environmental knowledge Scores between Rural and Urban Secondary School Students

Characteristic	Particulars	No. of Students	Environmental knowledge scores		Mean difference	t-value	P- value
			Mean	S D			
Locality	Rural	680	28.9	9.7	3.4	6.81*	<0.01
	Urban	834	32.3	10.0			

*Significant at 0.01 level of significance.

The obtained 't' value 6.81 is significant at 0.01 level of significance as it is more than the table value 2.58. Hence, the hypothesis is rejected.

Further, when means are compared, we can conclude that environmental knowledge of urban students (M = 32.3) is better than the rural students. (M = 28.9). The higher environmental knowledge of urban students is due to their better exposure to information via all kinds of media as well as their enhanced opportunities to experiment with nature and its components.

Sub Hypotheses

8.1-There is no significant difference in the environmental knowledge among the Rural and Urban secondary school Boys.

Table 4.17 : Significance of Difference in Mean Environmental knowledge Scores between the Boys of Rural and Urban Secondary Schools

Characteristic	Particulars	No. of Students	Environmental knowledge scores		Mean difference	t-value	P- value
			Mean	S D			
Boys	Rural	340	29.1	11.5	2.8	3.65*	< 0.01
	Urban	417	31.9	10.2			

*Significant at 0.01 level of significance.

It is evident from the table no 20, the obtained 't' value 3.65 is significant at 0.01 level of significance as it is more than the table value 2.58. Hence, the hypothesis is rejected.

Further, when means are compared, we can conclude that environmental knowledge of urban boys (M = 31.9) is better than the rural boys (M = 29.1). The higher scores made by urban boys were mainly because they were made environmentally sensitive as they are often the victims of degraded natural environment, and they were better informed as they were living in a world of better media net works. This difference is also due to the difference in the educational level of parents of urban and rural students.

Sub Hypotheses

8.2-There is no significant difference in the environmental Knowledge among the Rural and Urban secondary school Girls.

Table 4.18: Significance of Difference in Mean Environmental knowledge Scores between the Girls of Rural and Urban Secondary Schools

Characteristic	Particulars	No. of Students	Environmental knowladge scores		Mean difference	t-value	P-value
			Mean	S D			
Girls	Rural	340	28.7	7.6	4.1	6.27*	< 0.01
	Urban	417	32.8	9.9			

*Significant at 0.01 level of significance.

It is evident from the table no 21, the obtained 't' value 6.27 is significant at 0.01 level of significance as it is more than the table value 2.58. Hence, the hypothesis is rejected.

Further, when means are compared, we can conclude that environmental knowledge of urban girls (M = 32.8) is better than the rural girls (M = 28.7). The results obtained in this study are corroborated by the results obtained in the studies conducted by Sandhya Gihar (2006) and Kuhlemeia, H (1999).

Hypothesis-9

There is no significant difference in the environmental knowledge among the Students of Government and Private Secondary schools.

Table 4.19: Significance of Difference in Mean Environmental knowledge Scores between Government and Private Secondary School Students

Characteristic	Particulars	No. of Students	Environmental knowledge scores		Mean difference	t-value	P-value
			Mean	S D			
Types of Schools	Govt.	588	27.3	10.8	5.7	10.88*	< 0.01
	Private	848	33.0	9.0			

*Significant at 0.01 level of significance.

The data in the above table indicates that the, the obtained 't' value 10.88 is significant at 0.01 level of significance as it is more than the table value 2.58. Hence, the hypothesis is rejected.

Further, when means are compared, we can conclude that environmental knowledge of private school students (M = 33.0) is better than the students of government schools (M = 27.3). The findings thus revealed that private school students had developed more environmental knowledge than the government school students.

Sub Hypotheses

9.1-There is no significant difference in the environmental knowledge among the Boys of Govt. and Private Secondary schools.

It is evident from the table no 23, the obtained 't' value 3.48 is significant at 0.01 level of significance as it is more than the table value 2.58. Hence, the hypothesis is rejected.

Further, when means are compared, we can conclude that environmental knowledge of private school boys (M = 31.8) is better than the government school boys (M = 28.9).

Sub Hypotheses:

9.2-There is no significant difference in the environmental knowledge among the Girls of Government and private Secondary schools.

Table 4.21 : Significance of Difference in Mean Environmental knowledge Scores between the Girls of Government and Private Secondary Schools

Characteristic	Particulars	No. of Students	Environmental knowledge scores		Mean difference	t-value	P- value
			Mean	S D			
Girls	Govt.	294	25.7	7.3	8.6	13.58*	<0.01
	Private	424	34.3	8.9			

*Significant at 0.01 level of significance.

The findings in the table no, 24 shows that, the obtained 't' value 13.58 is significant at 0.01 level of significance as it is more than the table value 2.58. Hence, the hypothesis is rejected.

Further, when means are compared, we can conclude that environmental knowledge of girls of private schools (M = 34.3) is better than the girls of government schools (M = 25.7). This may be due to more opportunities given to private school students to become familiar with their environment and community centered co–curricular programmes in private schools.

Hypothesis-10

There is no significance interaction effect of sex and locality on environmental awareness.

The two way ANOVA details of scores of girls and boys of rural and urban secondary school with respect to environmental awareness of secondary schools of Davangere District are given in the following table,

The F-value of the above effect is 3.60 which is less than the table value 3.85 at 0.06 level. Hence it was concluded that the gender does not play an important role on environmental awareness of secondary school students. Hence the 1st null hypothesis is accepted.

Table 4.22 : Summary of Two way ANOVA of Sex and Locality on Environmental Awareness of secondary school students

Source	SS	df	MSS	F	P	F-table value
Between Gender	181	1	181.5	3.60	0.06	3.85
Between Locality	3002.4	1	3002.4	53.57	<0.01*	3.85
Interaction Gender X Locality	883.8	1	883.8	17.54	<0.01*	6.65
With in groups	72374.4	1436	50.4			
Total	76441.6	1439				

*Significant beyond the 0.01 level of probability.

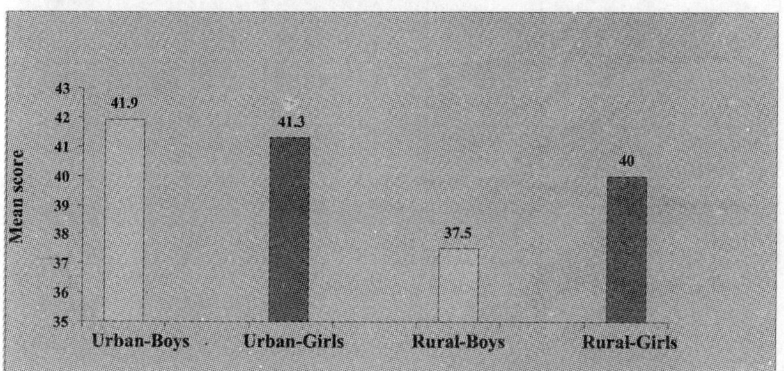

Fig. 4.1 : Interaction Effect of Gender and Locality on Environmental Awareness

The second null hypothesis of the effect of locality on environmental awareness is found to be significant as the F-ratio is found to be 53.57, which is significant at 0.01 levels. Hence it was concluded that, locality of the schools play an important role on environmental awareness of the secondary school students. Hence the 2nd hypothesis of the study is rejected.

The interactions of the variables, gender and locality of the schools is significant as the F- ratio is 17.54 which is also significant at 0.01 levels. From this it may be concluded that, gender and locality have joint effect on environmental awareness of the secondary school students. As a result the third hypothesis is rejected.

The results obtained in this study are corroborated by the results obtained in the studies conducted by Vipinder Sandhu and Jasvinder Singh Dillon (2005).

Hypothesis-11

There is no significance interaction effect of sex and types of secondary schools on environmental awareness.

Table 4.23: Summary of Two way ANOVA of Girls and Boys of Government and Private Secondary Schools Students with respect to Environmental Awareness

Source	SS	df	MSS	F	P	F-table value
Between Gender	115.4	1	115.4	2.17	0.14	3.85
Between Type o School	1148.0	1	1148.0	21.6	<0.01 *	6.65
Interaction, Gender X Type of School	25.3	1	25.3	0.48	0.49	3.85
With in groups	77476.8	1460	53.1	—		
Total	78765.5	1463				

*Significant beyond the 0.01 level of probability.

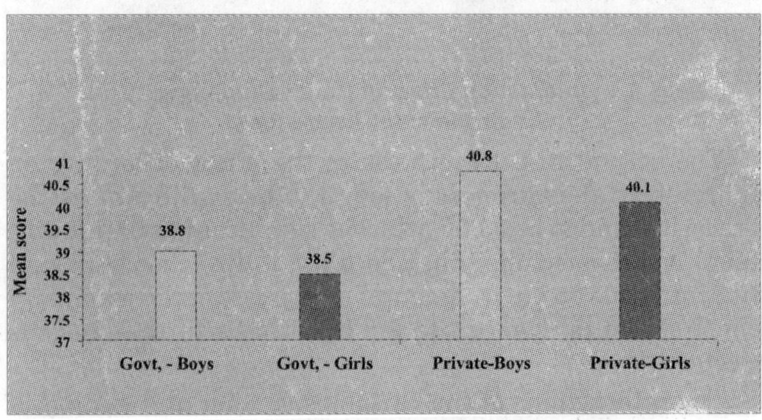

Fig. 4.2: Interaction Effect of Gender and Types of Schools on Environmental Awareness

The Two way ANOVA details of scores of girls and boys of government and private secondary schools with respect to environmental awareness of secondary school students of Davangere District are given in the following table.

The F-value of the above effect is 2.17 which is less than the table value 3.85 at 0.14 levels. Hence it was concluded that gender does not play any important role on environmental awareness. Hence the 1st null hypothesis is accepted. The third null hypothesis of the effect of type of school on environmental awareness is found to be significant as the F-ratio is 21.6 which is significant at 0.01 level. Hence it was concluded that, the type of schools play an important role on environmental awareness of the secondary school students. Hence third null hypothesis is rejected.

The interaction of variables, gender and type of school is not significant as the F- ratio is 0.48 which is less than the table value 3.85 at 0.49 level of significance. Hence it is concluded that gender and type of secondary school does not have any joint effect on environmental awareness of the secondary school students. Hence the above mentioned hypothesis is accepted.

The results obtained in this study are corroborated by the results obtained in the studies conducted by Chandrasekhar (2002).

Hypothesis-12

Table 4.24: Summary of 2 way ANOVA of Government and Private of Rural and Urban Secondary School students with respect to Environmental Awareness

Source	SS	df	MSS	F	P	F-table value
Between Locality	7659	1	7659	157.8	<0.0.1*	6.65
Between Type of School	1489	1	1488	30.7	<0.01*	6.65
Interaction Locality X Type of School	672	1	672	13.9	<0.01*	6.65
With in groups	71050	1464	48.5			
Total	80869	1467				

*Significant beyond the 0.01 level of probability.

There is no significance interaction effect of types of schools and locality on environmental awareness.

The 2 way ANOVA details of the scores of government and private, urban and rural secondary school students with respect to environmental awareness of secondary school students of Davangere District are given in following table.

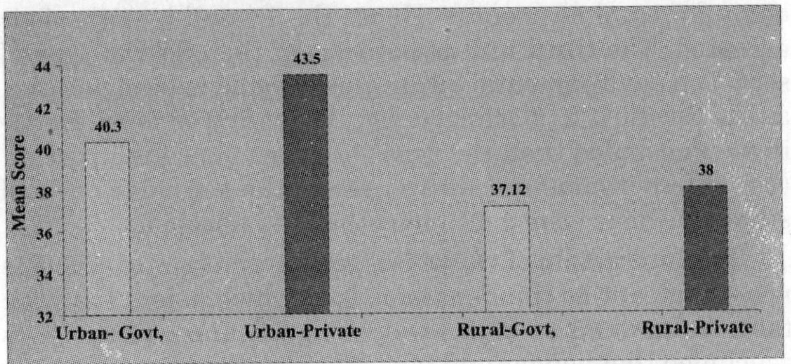

Fig. 4.3: Interaction Effect of Types of Schools and Locality on Environmental Awareness

The F-value of the above effect is 157.8 which is significant at 0.01 level. Hence it is concluded that, rural and urban secondary school students do play very important role on environmental awareness. Hence the 2nd null hypothesis is rejected.

The third null hypothesis of the effect of type of secondary school on environmental awareness is found to be significant as the F-ratio is 30.7 which is significant at 0.01 level. Hence it was concluded that, the type of secondary schools play an important role on environmental awareness of the secondary school students. Hence the third null hypothesis is rejected.

The interaction of variables, i.e. locality and types of schools is significant as the F-ratio is 13.9 which is more than the table value 6.65 and it is significant at 0.01 level. Hence it is concluded that the locality and type of school have joint effect on environmental awareness of secondary school students. Hence the above mentioned null hypothesis is rejected.

Hypothesis-13

There is no significance interaction effect of sex and locality on environmental attitude.

The 2 way ANOVA details of girls and boys of rural and urban secondary school students with respect to environmental attitude of secondary school students of Davangere District are given in the following table.

Table 4.25: Summary of the 2 way ANOVA of Girls and Boys of Rural and Urban Secondary School Students with respect to Environmental Attitude

Source	SS	df	MSS	F	P	F-table value
Between Gender	452	1	452	0.73	0.39Ns	3.85
Between Locality	42545	1	42545	68.3	<0.01*	6.65
Interaction Gender X Locality	190	1	190	0.30	0.58Ns	3.85
With in groups	913945	1466	623.4			
Total	957132	1469				

*Significant beyond the 0.01 level of probability.
Ns—Non-significant.

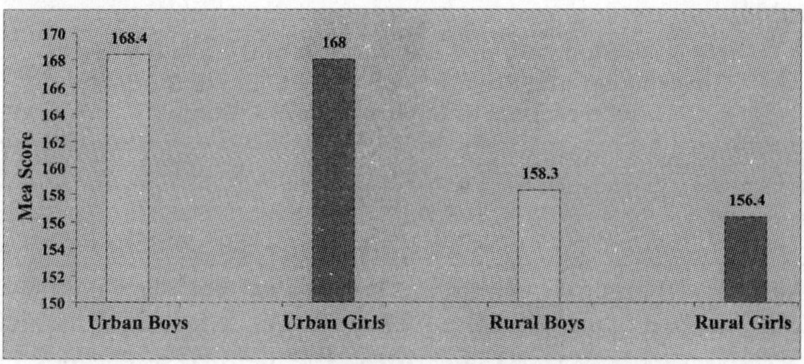

Fig. 4.4 : Interaction Effect of Gender and Locality on Environmental Attitude

The F-value of the above effect is 0.73 which is less than the table value 3.85. Hence it is concluded that the gender does not play an important role on environmental attitude of secondary school students. Hence the 4th null hypothesis of the study is accepted.

The 5th null hypothesis of the effect of locality on environmental attitude is found to be significant as the F-ratio is 68.3 which is significant at 0.01 level. Hence it was concluded that locality of the schools play an important role on environmental attitude of the secondary school students. Hence the 5th hypothesis is rejected.

The interaction of variables, gender and locality of schools is not significant as the F-ratio is 0.30 which is less than the table value 3.85. Hence it is concluded that gender and locality does not have any joint effect on environmental attitude of secondary school students as a result the above mentioned hypothesis is accepted.

Hypothesis-14

There is no significance interaction effect of sex and types of secondary schools on environmental attitude.

The 2 way ANOVA details of the scores of girls and boys of government and private secondary school students with respect to environmental attitude of secondary school students of Davangere District are given in the following table.

Table 4.26: Summary of 2 way ANOVA of Girls and Boys of Government and Private Secondary Schools Students with respect to Environmental Attitude

Source	SS	df	MSS	F	P	F-table value
Between Gender	1657	1	1657	2.37	0.12 Ns	3.85
Between Types of Schools	25182	1	25182	36.07	<0.01*	6.65
Interaction Gender X Types	2648	1	2648	3.79	0.06 Ns	3.85
With in groups	1022123	1464	698.2			
Total	1051613	1467				

*Significant beyond the 0.01 level of probability.

Ns—Non significant.

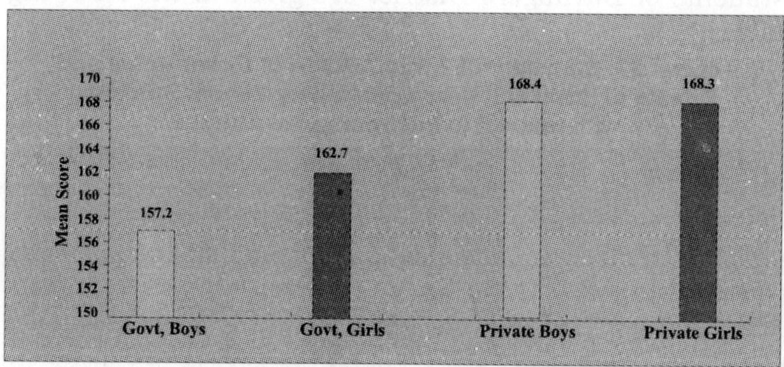

Fig. 4.5: Interaction Effect of Gender and Types of Schools on Environmental Attitude

The F-value of the above effect is 2.37 which is less than the table value 3.85 at 0.12 level. Hence it is concluded that gender does not play any important role on environmental attitude. Hence the 4th null hypothesis is accepted.

The 6th null hypothesis of the effect of type of secondary school on environmental attitude is found to be significant as the F-ratio is 36.07 which is significant at 0.01 level. Hence it was concluded that the type of secondary schools play an important role on environmental attitude of the secondary school students. Hence the 6th null hypothesis is rejected.

The interaction of variables, gender and type of schools is not significant as the F-ratio is 3.79 which is less than the table value 3.85 at 0.06 levels. Hence it is concluded that gender and type of secondary schools does not have any joint effect on environmental attitude of secondary school students. Hence the above mentioned hypothesis is accepted.

Hypothesis -15

There is no significance interaction effect of types of schools and locality on environmental attitude.

The 2 way ANOVA details of the scores of government and private, rural and urban secondary school students with respect to environmental attitude of the secondary school students of Davangere District are given in the following table.

Table 4.27: Summary of 2 way ANOVA of Government and Private of Rural and Urban Secondary School Students with respect to Environmental Attitude

Source	SS	df	MSS	F	P	F-table value
Between Locality	67432	1	67432	107.8	<0.01*	6.65
Between Types of Schools	25182	1	25182	40.3	<0.01*	6.65
Interaction Locality X Types	43109	1	43109	68.9	<0.01*	6.65
With in groups	915890	1464	625.6			
Total	1051613	1467				

*Significant beyond the 0.01 level of probability.

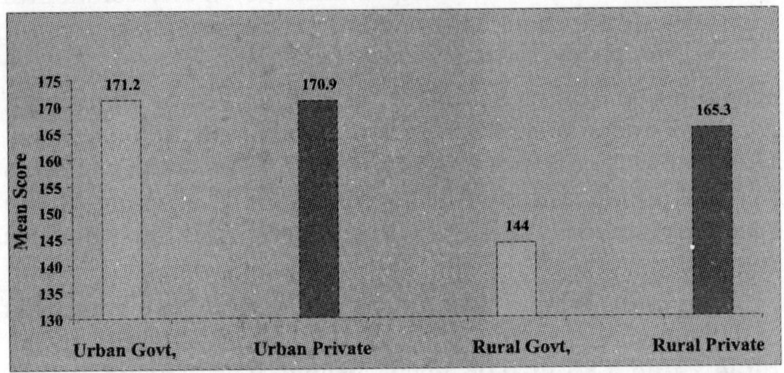

Fig. 4.6: Interaction Effect of Types of Schools and Locality on Environmental Attitude

The F-value of the above effect is 107.8 which is significant at 0.01 level. Hence it is concluded that locality of the school play a very important role on environmental attitude. Hence the 4th null hypothesis is rejected.

The 6th null hypothesis of the effect of type of secondary school on environmental attitude is found to be significant as the F- ratio is 40.3 which is significant at 0.01 levels.

Hence it was concluded that, the type of schools play an important role on environmental attitude of secondary school students. Hence the 6th null hypothesis is rejected.

The interaction of variables, i.e. rural and urban and type of school is significant as the F-ratio is 68.9 which is more than the table value 6.65 and it is significant at 0.01 levels. Hence it is concluded that the locality and type of schools have joint effect on environmental attitude of secondary school students. Hence the above mentioned null hypothesis is rejected.

Hypothesis-16

There is no significance interaction effect of sex and locality on environmental knowledge.

The 2 way ANOVA details of girls and boys of rural and urban secondary school students with respect to environmental knowledge of secondary school students are given in the following table.

Table 4.28: Summary of the 2 way ANOVA of Girl and Boys of Rural and Urban Secondary School Students with respect to Environmental Knowledge

Source	SS	df	MSS	F	P	F-table value
Between Gender	31.5	1	31.5	0.32	0.57Ns	3.85
Between Locality	3846.1	1	3846.1	38.30	<0.01*	6.65
Interaction Gender X Locality	172.0	1	172.0	1.72	0.18Ns	3.85
With in groups	147232.9	1466	100.4			
Total	151282.5	1469				

*Significant beyond the 0.01 level of probability
Ns-Non-significant

The F-value of the above effect is 0.32 which is less than the table value 3.85 at 0.57 levels. Hence it is concluded that the gender does not play an important role on environmental knowledge of secondary school students. Hence the 7th null hypothesis is accepted.

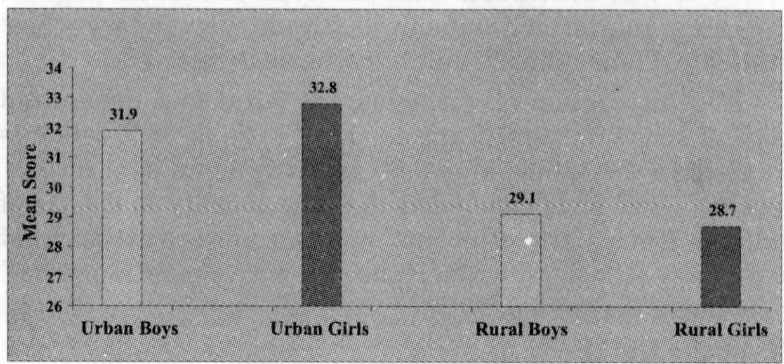

Fig. 4.7: Interaction Effect of Gender and Locality on Environmental Knowledge

The 8th null hypothesis of the effect of locality on environmental knowledge is found to be significant as the F-ratio is 38.30 which is significant at 0.01 level. Hence it was concluded that locality of the schools play an important role on environmental knowledge of the secondary school students. Hence the 8th hypothesis is rejected.

The interaction of variables, gender and locality of secondary school students is not significant as the F-ratio is 1.72 which is less than the table value 3.85. Hence it is concluded that gender and locality does not have any joint effect on environmental knowledge of secondary school students, as a result the above mentioned hypothesis is accepted.

Hypothesis-17

There is no significance interaction effect of sex and types of secondary schools on environmental knowledge.

The 2 way ANOVA details of the scores of girls and boys of government and private secondary school students with respect to environmental knowledge of secondary school students of Davangere District are given in the following table,

The F- value of the above effect is 0.24 which is less than the table value 3.85 at 0.62 level. Hence it is concluded that gender does not play any important role on environmental knowledge. Hence the 7th null hypothesis is accepted.

Table 4.29: Summary of 2 way ANOVA of Girls and Boys of Government and Private Secondary Schools Students with respect to Environmental Knowledge

Source	SS	df	MSS	F	P	F-table value
Between Gender	22.4	1	22.4	0.24	0.62Ns	3.85
Between Types of Schools	11360.3	1	11360.3	121.6	<0.01*	6.65
Interaction Gender X Types of Schools	2708.0	1	2708.0	29.0	<0.01*	6.65
With in groups	133389.6	1428	93.4	—		
Total	147480.3	1431				

*Significant beyond the 0.01 level of probability
Ns—Non-significant

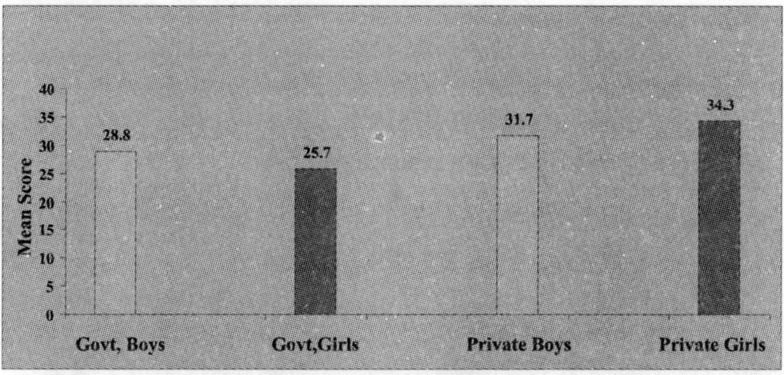

Fig. 4.8: Interaction Effect of Gender and Types of Schools on Environmental Knowledge

The 8th null hypothesis of the effect of type of schools on environmental knowledge is found to be significant as the F-ratio is 121.6 which is significant at 0.01 level. Hence it was concluded that the type of schools play an important role on environmental knowledge of the secondary school students. Hence the 8th null hypothesis is rejected.

The interaction of variable, gender and type of school is found to be significant as the F- ratio is 29.0 which is significant at 0.01 levels. Hence it is concluded that the gender and the types of schools have joint effect on environmental knowledge of secondary school students. Hence the above mentioned hypothesis is rejected.

Hypothesis-18

There is no significance interaction effect of types of schools and locality on environmental knowledge.

Table 4.30: Summary of 2 way ANOVA of Government and Private of Rural and Urban Secondary School Students with respect to Environmental Knowledge

Source	SS	df	MSS	F	P	F-table value
Between Locality	4598	1	4598	52.7	<0.01*	6.65
Between Types of Schools	12095	1	12095	138.6	<0.01*	6.65
Interaction, Locality X Types of Schools	6030	1	6030	69.1	<0.01*	6.65
With in groups	128484	1472	87.3			
Total	1561207	1475				

*Significant beyond the 0.01 level of probability.

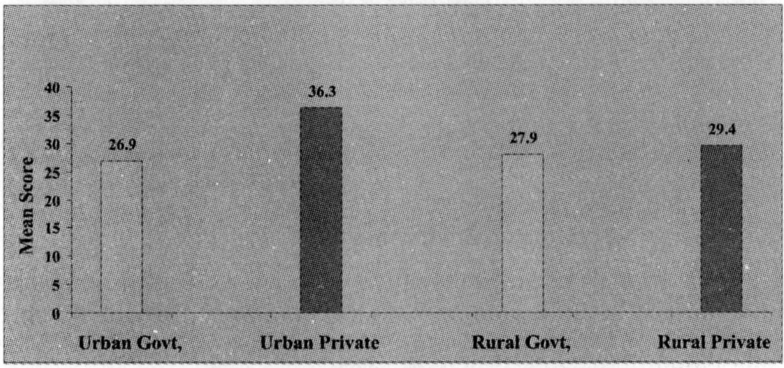

Fig. 4.9: Interaction Effect of Types of Schools and Locality on Environmental Knowledge

The 2 way ANOVA details of the scores of government and private, rural and urban secondary school students with respect to environmental knowledge of the secondary school students of Davangere District are given in the following table,

The F-value of the above effect is 52.7 which is significant at 0.01 level. Hence it is concluded that locality of the school do play a very important role on environmental knowledge. Hence the 8th null hypothesis is rejected.

The 9th null hypothesis of the effect of type of secondary schools on environmental knowledge is found to be significant as the F- ratio is 138.6 which is significant at 0.01 level. Hence it was concluded that, the type of school play an important role on environmental knowledge of the secondary school students. Hence the 9th null hypothesis is rejected.

The interaction of variables, i.e. locality and type of schools is significant as the F-ratio is 69.1 which is more than the table value 6.65 and it is significant at 0.01 level. Hence it is concluded that the locality and type of school have joint effect on environmental knowledge of secondary school students. Hence the above mentioned null hypothesis is rejected.

REFERENCES

1. Abraham, M and Arjun, N.K: *"Environmental Attitude and Pro-environmental Behaviour among Secondary School Children"*. Edutrack, Vol. 4. No. 6, pp.32-34
2. Aggarwal, Y.P: *"Statistical Methods, Concepts and Competition"*. 3rd Edition, Sterling Publishers (p) 2002. Ltd. New Delhi-20
3. Bruce W, Tuckman: *"Conducting Educational Research"*. Harcourt. Brace Jovanovich, Inc.1978, pp. 262-268.
4. Garett, Henry E: *"Statistics in Psychology and Education"*. Bombay: Vakils, Feffer and Simons Ltd., 1981, pp. 276-295.
5. Sahaya. Mary, I Paul Raj: *"Environmental Awareness among High School Students"*. Edutrack, 2005, pp. 33-35.

5

Summary of the Findings and Suggestions

In the previous chapter, the analysis and interpretation of data have been presented in detail. In this chapter, the researcher presents a brief summary of the research which indicates the statement of the problem, major objectives, hypotheses tested, methodology followed by the researcher, sampling and the tools and techniques used in the analysis of data. It also includes the conclusions drawn on the basis of interpretation of the findings, educational implications of the study and suggestions for further research.

Need and Importance of the Study

Till recently man was unaware of the fact that his technology is creating environmental imbalance, but now it has been realized that the earth's resources are finite and hence, are to be preserved and ecological balance must be maintained. The present problem of exploiting environment results largely from ignorance. The environmental problem has become one of the burning issues in our society, as people are not aware of environmental degradation. People need to be made aware of environment and its problems. They need to gain knowledge about how it functions, how human and the environment interact, how problems arise, and how they can be solved. They need to acquire about the environment and feel motivated and committed to repair, maintain and improve it.

The environmental problems have reached a level where almost everyone is conscious of them. This rising conscious has also given to a wide spread responsiveness of the idea for the need to do something about it. Education is obviously a powerful vehicle for bringing about change and there has been a growing interest in environmental education to serve the function. In act, environmental education at all levels of formal education was mandated by Supreme Court in 1991 in a response to public interest law suit on the need for action to create environmental awareness among the citizens of India.

Environmental problem exists in all countries and at all stages of development, but they vary in nature, magnitude and complexity. Environmental problems of developing countries are mostly related to improper modes of development and underdevelopment such as poverty, hunger, malnutrition and diseases. In developing countries, on the other hand, environmental problems rise due to fast development, which results in depletion of the resources, wastage of resources and pollution, India was an underdeveloped country and now being a developing country both these problems exists in India. The present environment is being degraded as a result of unsustainable exploitation of natural resources and environmental practices of human being. This is done in the form of mismanagement of natural environment, faulty practices, negative attitudes and deteriorating value structure in society. The agricultural and industrial revolution and subsequent modernization process have been responsible for the pollution and degradation of air, water, soil and with consequent adverse effect on human health and well being.

Environmental awareness is most important because people in developed countries are rapidly consuming earth's natural resources and because world population is increasing rapidly. Hence Human beings must take individual and social responsibility for the environment. It is pathetic to notice that younger generation of India is much behind in the concern for environmental balance. Therefore it is felt necessary to study the environmental awareness, attitude and knowledge among the secondary school students. It is very important to raise awareness among the teaching and student community. The awareness raising programmes are mostly concentrated around certain areas and the rest of the country is left out. Preparing the teaching community for effective integration of environmental concepts and creating positive attitudes in the young minds are greatly needed in every strata of the educational system. Unfortunately, the present efforts get diluted in the mad rush for academic achievements.

India faces significant challenges in protecting the environment from further damage. Population growth and urbanization make the task all the more difficult for the Indian government. It has made significant efforts in the field of environmental protection, and developing environmental standards for both products and processes. The Indian government's ability to safeguard the countries environment depends on polices and educational systems. The quality of life of people living in urban areas has declined considerably because of pollution. Protection of the environment is one of the major challenges facing the world. Hence human beings are asked to reduce, reuse and recycle their resources. Even the learned people do not know which object are to be reduced, reused and recycled. These three words if followed each and every person would be helpful to protect our environment.

Environmental education has been recognized all over the world as a viable tool for creating environmental awareness in people and motivating them to act for the environment. With the acceptance of Tiwari Committee Report in 1990, the country realized the need of environmental education. It is needed in order to meet the demand of every day life and maintain a mental equilibrium for the fulfillment of the needs and wants of every citizen on earth, and for balance and harmony between humanity and environment. It helps in developing new knowledge, skills and values in a drive towards better quality of life. It is needed for biomedical awareness and solution to health problems. A properly guided awareness is necessary to instill and enlighten the mind of Indians. Awareness leads to action. Without proper educational efforts the awareness analysis action chain does not move smoothly and effectively.

The relationship between environment and human kind is indeed deep and has been recognized from the Vedic period. Furthermore, non-violence towards both animate and inanimate components of biosphere has been ingrained as a guiding principle in the Indian psyche. Therefore, awareness and education of environment is the paramount concern of all the citizens of society. Environment protection starts by creating awareness among the people so that it becomes part of their lifestyle. The key to achieving this goal lies in environmental and its related programmes. The objective of environmental education includes awareness, knowledge, attitudes, skills and participation of people in protecting the environment.

The role of younger generation is crucial in achieving these objectives. Hence the investigator feels that, it is necessary to know about the awareness of younger generations about environment and environmental problems. In this present study, the researcher has made an attempt to analyse the environmental awareness, attitude and knowledge among secondary school students of different localities of Davangere District. The investigator has tried to identify the environmental awareness, attitude and knowledge among the secondary school students and studied the relationship of the environmental awareness, attitude and knowledge among the Boys and Girls, Urban and Rural, Government and Private secondary school students of Davangere District.

The proposed study will be confined to the secondary school (9th standard) students presently studying in

Davangere District as they will be in the middle of the secondary education. 8th standard students are fresh for high school education as they have come from primary education. They are lacking in the basic concepts of environment. Hence they are not selected as sample. Even 10th standard students are not selected as sample because they will be busy in preparing for the board examinations and also the lack of cooperation from the heads of the schools. Hence the sample covers randomly selected rural and urban secondary school (9th standard) students of Davangere District.

Statement of the Problem

The problem of the present study is *"An Investigation into the Environmental Awareness, Attitude and Knowledge among the Secondary School Students of Davangere District"*.

Objectives of the Study

The present study was undertaken with the following broad objectives:

(*i*) To identify the environmental awareness among the secondary school students

(*ii*) To identify the environmental attitude among the secondary school students.

(*iii*) To identify the environmental knowledge among the secondary school students.

(*iv*) To suggest measures to develop environmental awareness, attitude and knowledge among the secondary school students of Davangere District.

Specific Objectives of the Study

(*a*) To find out the environmental awareness among the secondary school Boys and Girls of Davangere District.

(*b*) To find out the environmental awareness among the Rural and Urban Secondary school Boys and Girls of Davangere District.

(*c*) To find out the environmental awareness among the secondary school Boys and Girls of Government and Private secondary schools of Davangere District.

(*d*) To find out the environmental Attitude among the secondary school Boys and Girls of Davangere District.

(*e*) To find out the environmental Attitude among the Rural and Urban Secondary school Boys and Girls of Davangere District.

(*f*) To find out the environmental Attitude among the secondary school Boys and Girls of Government and Private secondary schools of Davangere District.

(*g*) To find out the environmental knowledge among the secondary school Boys and Girls of Davangere District.

(*h*) To find out the environmental knowledge among the Rural and Urban Secondary school Boys and Girls of Davangere District.

(*i*) To find out the environmental knowledge among the secondary School Boys and Girls of Government and Private secondary schools of Davangere District.

(*j*) To find out the interaction effect of Sex and Locality on Environmental awareness, attitude and knowledge of secondary school students.

(*k*) To find out the interaction effect of Sex and Types of schools on Environmental awareness, attitude and knowledge of secondary school students.

(*l*) To find out the interaction effect of Locality and Types of school on Environmental awareness, attitude and knowledge of secondary school students.

Hypotheses Tested

Based upon the discussions of variables and also keeping in view the objectives of the study, the following research hypotheses have been formulated.

1. There is no significant difference in the environmental awareness among the secondary school Boys and Girls.
2. There is no significant difference in the environmental awareness among the Rural and Urban Secondary school students.

   Sub Hypotheses

   2.1. There is no significant difference in the environmental awareness among the Rural and Urban secondary school Boys.

   2.2. There is no significant difference in the environmental awareness among the Rural and Urban secondary school Girls.
3. There is no significant difference in the environmental awareness among the students of Govt, and Private Secondary schools.

   Sub Hypotheses

   3.1. There is no significant difference in the environmental awareness among the Boys of Govt, and Private Secondary schools.

   3.2. There is no significant difference in the environmental awareness among the Girl students of Govt, and Private Secondary schools.
4. There is no significant difference in the environmental attitude among the secondary school Boys and Girls.
5. There is no significant difference in the environmental attitude among the Rural and Urban Secondary school students.

   Sub Hypotheses

   5.1. There is no significant difference in the environmental attitude among the Rural and Urban secondary school Boys students.

   5.2. There is no significant difference in the environmental attitude among the Rural and Urban secondary school Girls.

6. There is no significant difference in the environmental attitude among the Students of Government and Private Secondary schools.

Sub Hypotheses

6.1. There is no significant difference in the environmental attitude among the Boys of Govt, and Private Secondary schools.

6.2. There is no significant difference in the environmental attitude among the Girl students of Govt, and Private Secondary schools.

7. There is no significant difference in the environmental knowledge among the secondary school Boys and Girls.

8. There is no significant difference in the environmental knowledge among the Rural and Urban Secondary school students.

Sub Hypotheses

8.1. There is no significant difference in the environmental knowledge among the Rural and Urban secondary school Boys.

8.2. There is no significant difference in the environmental knowledge among the Rural and Urban secondary school Girls.

9. There is no significant difference in the environmental knowledge among the Students of Government and Private Secondary schools.

Sub Hypotheses

9.1. There is no significant difference in the environmental knowledge among the Boys of Government and Private Secondary schools.

9.2. There is no significant difference in the environmental knowledge among the Girl students of Government and Private Secondary schools.

10. There is no significance interaction effect of sex and locality on environmental awareness.
11. There is no significance interaction effect of sex and types of secondary schools on environmental awareness.
12. There is no significance interaction effect of types of schools and locality on environmental awareness
13. There is no significance interaction effect of sex and locality on environmental attitude.
14. There is no significance interaction effect of sex and types of secondary schools on environmental attitude.
15. There is no significance interaction effect of types of schools and locality on environmental attitude.
16. There is no significance interaction effect of sex and locality on environmental knowledge.
17. There is no significance interaction effect of sex and types of secondary schools on environmental knowledge.
18. There is no significance interaction effect of types of schools and locality on environmental knowledge.

Methodology and Sampling

In the present study, the data regarding independent variables such as secondary school boys and girls, urban and rural secondary school students, government and private secondary school 9th standard students of Davangere District was collected.

The investigator has used the following tools for the collection of the data.

1. Environmental Awareness Ability Measure (Praveen Kumar Jha, 1998)
2. Taj Environmental Attitude Scale (Haseen Taj, 2001)
3. Environmental Knowledge Test constructed by the researcher was used to investigate the Environmental Knowledge among the secondary school students.

Sampling

For the purpose of present study, 1440 students were selected from the 9th standard classes of Davangere District. Stratified random sampling technique was used to select the sample. Totally 36 secondary schools were selected proportionately on random basis; 14 were government secondary schools and 22 were private secondary schools. Among the 14 government schools, 7 were urban government secondary schools and remaining 7 were of rural government secondary schools.

Among the 22 private secondary schools, 12 were urban private secondary schools and 10 were rural private secondary schools. The proportion of the sample of urban and rural secondary school students is almost in the ratio of 1:1 (770:680); boys and girls sample is also in the ratio of 1:1(720:720).

Statistical techniques used for the analysis of the data

The researcher has used the following statistical techniques for the analysis of the data - Mean, and Standard Deviations were calculated for the scores in the groups, test of significance i.e. paired-'t' test was calculated to compare the independent variables in between the groups. The hypotheses formulated were tested using the-Two way ANOVA.

Findings and Conclusions of the Study

The following are the findings of the present study,

1. Gender does not play any role on Environmental awareness.
2. Localities of the schools play an important role on environmental awareness.
3. Gender and locality have joint effect on environmental awareness.
4. Gender and types of schools does not have any joint effect on environmental awareness.

5. Types of secondary schools play an important role on environmental awareness.
6. Locality and type of schools have joint effect on environmental awareness.
7. Gender does not play an important role on environmental attitude.
8. Localities of the schools play an important role on environmental attitude.
9. Gender and locality does not have any joint effect on environmental attitude.
10. Types of secondary school play an important role on environmental attitude.
11. Gender and type of secondary school does not have any joint effect on environmental attitude.
12. Locality and type of school have joint effect on environmental attitude.
13. Gender does not play an important role on environmental knowledge.
14. Localities of the schools play an important role on environmental knowledge.
15. Gender and locality does not have any joint effect on environmental knowledge.
16. Types of schools play an important role on environmental knowledge.
17. Gender and type of schools have joint effect on environmental knowledge.
18. Locality and type of schools have joint effect on environmental knowledge.

Conclusions

The researcher has drawn the following conclusions on the basis of interpretations of results which are as follows,

1. Lack of better exposure to information via all kinds of media is the cause of lower environmental awareness in the rural students.

2. Meagre opportunities to become familiar with the environment and community centered co-curricular programmes in government schools is the cause of lower environmental attitude among the students of government schools.
3. Lack of concrete concepts about environmental aspects and less polluted environment in rural areas is the cause of lower environmental knowledge among rural students.
4. A lower education level of parents in rural areas is also one of the causes of lower environmental awareness, attitude and knowledge among the rural students.

Educational Implications of the Study

The following educational implications may be suggested based on the results obtained in the study.

1. Environmental awareness, attitude and knowledge are significantly and positively related to locality of the schools. Lower environmental awareness, attitude and knowledge of the students in rural areas are due to lack of better exposure to information via all kinds of media. Hence they must be provided better opportunities to gather information regarding environment by conducting symposiums, seminars and exhibitions.

R Sahaya Mary and I Paul raj, (15:33-35). Ramakrishnanan, A (16:78-90), Abraham and Arjuna, N.K (3:32-34), Bradly, J.C, Waliczek, T.M & Zajicck, T.M (5:17-21), have found that Environmental awareness is influenced by the locality of the schools.

2. The results of the study indicate that the students belonging to urban background are comparatively better in terms of their environmental awareness, attitude and knowledge as compared to the student belonging to rural back ground. This difference is due to the difference in the educational level of the parents of urban and rural students

and the approaches of the media is also an important factor and also the poor environmental quality in urban areas leads to individuals facing serious health problems. Hence individuals adopt measures to improve their environment quality only if they perceive the associated health problems.

Bapat, M.N and Nagaraja Rao, N.R (4:10-19), Gutteling, J.M and Weigman, O (7:433-447), Legault, et, al (11:243-250), Arcury, T and E, Christianson (2:19-25), Shahnawaj have found that students belonging to urban background are comparatively better in terms of their environmental awareness, attitude and knowledge as compared to the student belonging to rural back ground.

3. The study revealed that, environmental awareness, attitude and knowledge are significantly and positively related to types of schools. Lower environmental awareness, attitude and knowledge of government school students are due to lack of better facilities.

Hence it is very important to arrange community activity programmes and make students to actively participate in it. Government and other policy makers should invite authors, field workers and artists to work with creativity to produce special modules to promote environmental awareness, attitude and knowledge.

Makki, M.H and Abd-El-Khalick, F (12:21-33), Rane, A.J, (14), Blocker, I.J and Eckberg, D.T,(6:841-858), have found that environmental awareness, attitude and knowledge in government school students can be enhanced by active involvement of students in community activity programmes and also by developing special modules to develop environmental awareness, attitude and knowledge.

4. The environmental education syllabus must be brought near to the day to day life situations. Gihar, S, Saxena, M.K and Kukrethi, B.R (8:69-74) have found that successful environmental education must be activity based and investigative as well as case discussions and action projects must be involved in the education syllabus.

5. Training for government schools students and teachers must be given top priority and programmes may be chalked out accordingly. Praharaj, B (13) has found that by using new strategies or promoting new methodologies in government schools both for the students and teachers is very important to enhance environmental awareness, attitude and knowledge.

6. Teachers must be given special orientations with updated strategies. Gardos et al (9:1121-1122)

7. Students must be provided with more play way type of activities in Environmental Education like motivating them to develop some projects about the environment where they are living. Gopal Krishna, (10) & Jain, S.C (18:26-32).

8. Role of children's family is important on Environmental Educational Process, hence it is very important to arrange environmental educational seminars for parents.

9. Eco club activities must be strengthened as they play an important role in creating environmental awareness, attitude and knowledge amongst the future generation in the following ways,

(*i*) They are responsible for motivating the students to keep their surroundings green and clean by undertaking plantation of trees.

(*ii*) They can also promote ethos of conservation of water by minimizing the use of water.

(*iii*) To motivate students to imbibe habits and life style for minimum waste generation, source separation of waste and disposing the waste to the nearest storage point and also about re-use of waste material and preparation of products out of waste.

(*iv*) To educate students to create awareness amongst public and sanitary workers, so as to stop the indiscriminate burning of waste as this causes respiratory diseases.

(*v*) To sensitize the students to minimize the use of plastic bags, not to throw them in public places as they choke drains and sewers, cause water logging and provide breeding ground for mosquitoes.

(*vi*) To organize tree plantation programmes, awareness programmes such as Quiz, essay, painting competitions, poster competitions, rallys, natak etc. etc. so as to create enthusiasm regarding issues pertaining to Plants,Forest,Wildlife,Bio-diversity and Nature.

(*vii*) To organize Nature Trail in Wild Life Sanctuaries, Parks, Forest areas to know about the Bio-diversity.

10. Orientation programmes for Eco Club in charge teachers can be conducted with the help of Environment experts.

Limitations of the Study

1. The sample included the 9th standard students of Davangere District.
2. Sample covers the randomly selected rural and urban secondary school students of Davangere District.
3. Though a number of variables are related to environment; only a relationship of variables such as environmental awareness, environmental attitude and environmental knowledge were studied.

Suggestions for Further Research

1. Comprehensive studies on similar lines may be conducted to develop Environmental attitude by taking more variables like, Environmental Ethics, Air pollution attitude, Temperature attitude, Noise attitude, Noise sensitivity, Noise adaptation, Ecological attitude, Environmental values, Environmental behaviour. Etc
2. Similar studies can be conducted at different levels such as primary as well as in college levels.
3. Similar studies can also be conducted in different localities of other Districts.

4. A comparative study of interaction effects of the selected variables among the students studying in state board and C B S E syllabus can be undertaken
5. An experimental studies can be conducted with innovative methods such as Brain storming, Infusion approach as an independent variable to develop Environmental Attitude at college levels.

REFERENCES

1. Arjuna, N.K and Harikrishna, K: *"Environmental Attitude among Rural and Urban students"*. International Educator.11. 1 & 2. 1996, pp.20-22.
2. Arcury, T and E, Christianson: *"Rural and Urban Sstudents in Environmental Knowledge and Activity"*. Journal of Environmental Education. 25, pp.19-25.
3. Abraham and Arjuna, N.K: *"Environmental Attitude and Pro-environmental Behavior Among Secondary School Students"*. Edutracks. Feb 2005, vol No. 6, pp.32-34.
4. Bapat, M.N and Nagaraja Rao, N.R: *"Environmental Education at Primary level-Why and How?"* The Primary Teacher, NCERT Publications, New Delhi-16. (April 2004), Vol. xxix, No. 2, pp.10-19.
5. Bradly, J.C, Waliczek, T.M & Zajicck, T.M: *"Relationship between Demographic Variables and Environmental Attitude of High School Students"*. Journal of Environmental Education, 30(3), pp.17-21.
6. Blocker, I.J and Eckberg, D.T: *"Gender and Environmentalism; Results from the 1993. General Social Survey"* Social Science, Quarterly, 78, pp. 841-858.
7. Gutteling, J.M and Weigman, O: *"Hazards in the Netherlands"*. Sex Roles, 1993. Vol. 28, pp. 433-447.
8. Gihar, S. Saxena, M.K and Kukrethi,B.R: *"Developing Environmental Friendly Behavior among Students; Role of Video Intervention"* University News, 44 (12), March 20-26, pp. 69-74.
9. Gardos et al: *"An Immediate Response to Environmentally Disturbing News and Environmental Attitudes of College Students"*. Psychology Reports, Vol. 77 (3), pp. 1121-1122.
10. Gopal Krishna: *"Impact of Environmental Education on Primary School Children in Avinashilingam"*. Fifth Survey of Educational Research, Vol. II.

11. Legault, et, al: *"Impact of an Environmental Education Programme On Students and Parents, Attitudes, Motivation and Behavior".* Journal of Behavioral Science, Vol. 32(4), pp. 243-250.
12. Makki, M.H and Abd-El-Khalick, F: *"Lebanese Secondary School Students Environmental Knowledge and Attitudes".* Environmental Educational Research, Vol. 9, Jan. 2003, pp. 21-33.
13. Praharaj, B: *"Environmental Knowledge, Environmental Attitude and Perception Regarding Environmental Education among Pre-Service and in Service Secondary School Teacher".* Ph.D. Education, Maharaja Sayaji Rao, Baroda University.
14. Rane, A.J: *"Evaluation of Environmental Studies Approach of Parisar Asha in Municipal Schools in Greater Bombay".* 1989. Tata Institute of Social Science.
15. R. Sahaya Mary and I Paul raj: *"Environmental Awareness among High School Students".* Edutracks, December 2005, pp. 33-35.
16. Ramakrishna, A: *"A study of Environmental Awareness Among High School students".* School Science, NCERT Publications, New Delhi-June 2003, Vol. XLI, No. 2, pp. 78-90.
17. Shahnawaj: *"A Study of Environmental Awareness and Environmental Attitude on Secondary, Higher Secondary School Teachers and Students".* Ph.D Thesis in Education. University of Rajasthan, Jaipur, 1990.
18. Jain, S.C: *"Environmental Education in Nigerian Schools".* Educational Journal of India May 1990, pp. 26-32.

Bibliography

1. Abraham, M and Arjunun, N.K: *"Environmental Attitude and Pro–Environmental Behaviour among Secondary School Children"*. Edutracks, Vol. 4, No. 6, pp.32-34
2. Archi, M: *"Excellence in Environmental Education: Guidelines for Learning"* (K-10). Washington, D C: North American Association for Environmental Education, 2009.
3. Archi,M: *"Five Years of Advancing Education and Environmental Literacy"*. Washington, D.C: *North American Association for Environmental Education,* 2001.
4. Arcury, Thomas, A: *"Environmental Attitude and Knowledge"* Human Organisation. 49 (4), 1990.
5. Aggarwal, Y.P: "*Statistical Methods, Concepts and Competition"*. 3rd Edition. Sterling Publishers (p) 2002. Ltd. New Delhi-20.
6. Arcury, T and E, Christianson: *"Rural and Urban Students in Environmental Knowledge and Activity"*. Journal of Environmental Education. 25, pp.19-25.
7. Armstrong, J., & Impara, J: *"The Impact of an Environmental Education Programme on Knowledge and Attitude"*. Journal of Environmental Education, 2 (4), 1991, pp. 36-40.
8. Arjuna, N.K and Harikrishna, K: *"Environmental Attitude among Rural and Urban Students"*. International Educator. 11. 1 & 2. 1996, pp. 20-22.
9. Ayiashabi, T.C: *"Environmental Literacy of Science and Non-Science Students at Degree Level"*. Journal of All India Association for Educational Research.vol.II, No, 1&2, March 1999, pp. 23-39.
10. Balkrishna P: *"A Study on Environmental Knowledge, Environmental Attitude and Perception Regarding Environmental Education among Preservice and In-service Secondary School Teachers.* Thesis (Ph.D) M. S. University, Baroda, 1991
11. Bapat, M.N. and Nagaraja Rao, N.R: *"Environmental Education at Primary level-Why and How?"* The Primary Teacher, NCERT Publications, New Delhi-16. (April 2004), Vol. xxix, No. 2, pp.10-19.

12. Belgrade: *"Character Environmental Education Network"*. Washington.D.C. NAEE, 1976.
13. Bhanumathi, R: *"Environmental Education Strategies and Approaches"* in Environmental Issues, New Delhi; Reliance Publishing House, 2003.
14. Bradly, J.C, Waliczek, T.M & Zajicck, T.M: *"Relationship between Demographic Variables and Environmental Attitude of High School Students"*. Journal of Environmental Education, 30(3), pp.17-21.
15. Blocker, I.J and Eckberg, D.T: *"Gender and Environmentalism; Results from the 1993. General Social Survey"* Social Science, Quarterly, 78, pp.841-858.
16. Bruce W, Tuckman: "*Conducting Educational Research",* Harcourt, Brace Jovanovich, Inc. 1978, pp. 262-268.
17. Deshibandu: *"Environmental Education for Sustainable Development"*. India Environmental Society, New Delhi, 1995.
18. Desinger, J.F: *"What Research Says: Environmental Education"* The Ecologist, Vol. 85. 1985, pp.10-28.
19. Ebel, Robert L. and Frisble David A: *"Essentials of Educational Measurement"*. Fifth Edition, New Delhi: Prentice Hall of India Private Limited, 1991, pp. 228.
20. Edwin Harper. Erika. S. Harper: *"Preparing Objective Examinations: A Handbook for Teachers, Students and Examiners"*. Prentice Hall of India Private Limited, New Delhi, 1992.
21. Elvan Alp et al: *"A Statistical Analysis of Children's Environmental Knowledge and Attitudes in Turkey"*. International Research in Geographical and Environmental Education. Vol. 15. No, 3, 2006, pp.210–223.
22. Essential Learning's in Environmental Education: *"A Hand Book of Environmental Concepts"*, Brought out by Centre for Environmental Education, Ahamedabad, 1991.
23. Exemmal: *"Construction of Certain Models for Teaching Botany using Environmental and Ethnic Resources and Testing the Efficacy of Such Models. Ph.D Thesis.* University of Kerala.1980.
24. Garret, Henry E: *"Statistics in Psychology and Education*". Bombay Vakils, Feffer and Simons Pvt, Ltd., 1981, pp. 151-181.
25. Gardos et al: *"An Immediate Response to Environmentally disturbing News and Environmental Attitudes of College Students"*. Psychology Reports. Vol. 77 (3), pp.1121-1122.
26. Glenn, J.L: *"Environmental-based Education: Creating high Performance Schools and Students"*. Washington, DC: The National Environmental Education and Training *Foundation.* 2000.

27. Gopal Chandra. Pradhan: "*Environmental Awareness among Teacher Trainees*". University News, 1995, pp.10-16.

28. Grounlund Norman E: *"Measurement and Evaluation in Teaching"*. Third Edition, New York: Mac Milan Publishing Co., Inc., 1976, pp-285.

29. Gihar, S. Saxena, M.K and Kukrethi, B.R: *"Developing Environmental Friendly Behavior among Students; Role of Video Intervention"* University News, 44 (12), March 20-26. pp. 69-74.

30. Guilford, J.P: *"Fundamental Statistics in Psychology and Education"*. Fourth Eedition, New York: Mc Graw Hill Book Company, 1965, pp. 368.

31. Gutteling, J.M and Weigman, O: *"Hazards in the Netherlands"*. Sex Roles, 1993, Vol. 28, pp. 433-447.

32. Gopal Krishna: *"Impact of Environmental Education on Primary School Children in Avinashilingam"*. Fifth Survey of Educational Research, Vol. II.

33. Hans Kuhlemeier, Huub Van Den Bergh, Nijs Lagerweij: *"Environmental Knowledge, Attitudes and Behavior in Dutch Secondary Education"*. Journal of Environmental Education, Vol. 30, 1999.

34. Haseen Taj: *"Manual for Taj Environmental Attitude Scale"* TEAS, Agra; Nandini Enterprises, 2001, pp. 1-13.

35. Harper, Charles L: *"Environment and Society":* Human Perspectives on Environmental Issues, Printce Hill, New Jersey, 1996.

36. Ifegbesan Ayodeji: *"Student's Perceptions of Environmental Education Elements in Nigerian Junior Secondary School Curriculum"*. Perspectives in Education, vol. 18, No.1, pp. 59-64. 2003.

37. Jain, S.C: *"Environmental Education in Nigerian Schools"*. Educational Journal of India May 1990, pp.26-32.

38. Jennifer Campbell Bradley, T. M. Waliczek, and J. M. Zajicek: *"Relationship between Environmental Knowledge and Environmental Attitude of High School Students"*. Journal of Environmental Education, Vol. 30, 1999.

39. Joe E, Heimlich: "*Thesaurus of Environmental Education Terms. Columbus*". The Ohio State University, North American Association for Environmental Education (NAAEE).1999, pp. 1-5.

40. John W Best and James V Kahn: *"Research in Education"*. Prentice Hall of India Pvt. Ltd., New Delhi.

41. Kukreti, B.R.: *"Environmental Education: A Blue Print"*. University News, 31(43), 1993, pp.11-14.
42. Legault, et, al: *"Impact of an Environmental Education Programme on Students and Parents, Attitudes, Motivation and Behavior"*. Journal of Behavioral Science, Vol, 32(4). pp. 243-250.
43. Lokesh Koul: *"Methodology of Educational Research"*. Vikas Publishing House Pvt. Ltd. 2000.
44. Maryam Larijani and Yeshodhara k: *"Relationship between Environmental Attitude* and *Environmental Awareness among Higher Primary School Teachers of India and Iran"*. Journal of all India Association for Educational Research Vol.18, No. 3 & 4 September & December 2006.
45. Makki, M.H and Abd-El-Khalick, F: *"Lebanese Secondary School Students Environmental Knowledge and Attitudes"*. Environmental Educational Research. Vol. 9, Jan. 2003, pp.21-33.
46. Mathlow Ediger: *"Environmental Education, Teacher and the Student"*. Experiments in Education. 2007. pp.17-19.
47. Mercy Abraham and N.K. Arjunan: *"Environmental Interest of Secondary School Students in Relation to their Environmental Attitude"*. Perspectives in Education, Vol. 21, No. 2, 2005. pp.100-105.
48. Ministry of Human Resource Development: *"Environmental Education in National Policy Documents"*. 1992.
49. Mohua Guha and Aparajita Chattopadhyay: *" Environmental Education: A Pathway for Sustainable Development"*. Environmental Issues. New Delhi. Reliance Publishing House.
50. Murat Gokdere: *"A Study on Environmental Knowledge Level of Primary Students in Turkey"*. Asia–Pacific Forum on Science Learning and Teaching". Vol. 6, Issue 2, Article 5, December 2005.
51. Narasimha Reddy, D: "*Sustainable Development*". Edutracks. 2002. pp.35-37.
52. NCERT: *"Curriculum Frame work for Teacher Education"*. New Delhi, National Council of Educational Research and Training, 2004.
53. NCERT: *"National Consultations on Environmental Education In Schools"*. New Delhi, National Council of Educational Research and Training, 2000.
54. Patel, D.G. Patel, N.: "*An Investigation into the Environmental Awareness and its Enhancement in the Secondary School Teachers"*. Progress of Education. 766(12), 1995, pp. 256-257.

55. Paraskevopoulos, S: Zafiropoulos:*"Environmental Knowledge of Elementary School Students in Greece"*. Journal of Environmental Education, Vol. 29, 1998.

56. Praveen Kumar Jha: *"Manual for Environmental Awareness Ability Measure"* (EAAM), Agra; National Psychological Corporation, 1998, pp.1-19.

57. Pradhan, G.C: *"Environmental Awareness among the Secondary School Teachers"*. Experiments in Education, 2002, pp.03-05.

58. Praharaj, B: *"Environmental Knowledge, Environmental Attitude and Perception Regarding Environmental Education among Pre-service and in Service Secondary School Teacher"*. Ph.D. Education. Maharaja Sayaji Rao, Baroda University.

59. Rajasrhi Roy, et al: *"Attitude of the Undergraduate Pharmacy Students Towards Environmental Awareness"*. Journal of All India Association for Educational Research, Vol. 18, No. 3 & 4, September 2006, pp.87-93.

60. Ramakrishna, A: *"A Study of Environmental Awareness Among High School Students"*. School Science, NCERT Publications, New Delhi-June 2003, Vol. XLI, No. 2, pp.78-90.

61. Rane, A.J: *"Evaluation of Environmental Studies Approach of Parisar Asha in Municipal Schools in Greater Bombay"*. 1989. Tata Institute of Social Science.

62. Rusky, A., Wilke, R., & Beasly: *"T. A Survey of the Status of State-Level Environmental Education in the United States"*-1998 update. Journal of Environmental Education. 2001.

63. Santhosh kumar Rout, Sukirti Agarwal: *"Environmental Awareness and Environmental Attitude of Students at High School Level"*. Edutracks. 2006, Vol. 6 (1), pp.25-26.

64. Sandhya Gihar: *"Environmental Responsibility among Students"*. Edutracks, Vol.6, No.1, September 2006, pp.27-32.

65. Sahaya Mary, I Paul Raj: *"Environmental Awareness among High School Students"*. Edutracks. December 2005, pp. 33-35.

66. Sharma, R.C and Merle, C Tan: *"Source Book in Environmental Education for Secondary School Teachers"*. UNESCO, Bangkok, 1992.

67. Sharma, R.C: *"Implications of Environmental Education in Teacher Education"*. Journal of Indian Education. 2004, pp.5-13.

68. Sreekumari, K.E ands Ajitha,K: *"Environmental Awareness of Secondary School Children of Kerala"*. International Educator, 13:1 & 2, 1998, pp.41-46.

69. Shobeiri,S.M.,Omiidvar,B.and Prahallada,N.N: *"A Comparative Study of Environmental Awareness among Secondary School Students in Iran and India"* International Journal of Environmental Research, Vol. 1, No. 1, 2007, pp.28-34.
70. Shahnawaj: *"A Study of Environmental Awareness and Environmental Attitude on Secondary, Higher Secondary School Teachers and Students"*. Ph.D Thesis in Education. University of Rajasthan, Jaipur, 1990.
71. Smith Sebasto N J: *"Potential Guide lines for Conducting and Reporting Environmental Educational Research"*. Qualitative Methods of Inquiry, Vol.II, 2000, pp.9-26.
72. Shivakumar,K. Mangala, S. Patil: *"Influence of Environmental Education on Environmental Attitude of the Post-Graduate Students"*, Edutracks, Vol.6, No.8, April 2007, pp.34-36.
73. Tan Geok-Chin Ivy et al: *"A Survey of Environmental Knowledge, Attitudes and Behaviour of Students in Singapore"*. International Research in Geographical and Environmental Education Vol.7, No. 3, 1998, pp.181-195.
74. Thorndike, R: *"Personal Selection Test and Measurement Techniques"*, New York: John Wiley and Sons Inc., February, 1996, pp.245.
75. Tuckman, Bruce W: *"Conducting Educational Research"*. New York: Harcourt Brace Jovanovich Inc., 1978, pp. 58-59.
76. Vijayalakshmi, S: *"Environmental Education: Concern and Strategies"* in Environmental Issues. New Delhi; Reliance Publishing House, 2003.
77. Wheeler, K: *"The Genesis of Environmental Education"*, in Insights into Environmental Education, ed. G.C. Martin and K.Wheeler (Edinburgh: Oliver and Boyd, 1975, pp. 4.
78. William,E. Marden:*"Environmental Education, Historical Roots, Comparative, Perspective and Current Issues in Britain and United States"*. Perspectives in Education Vol. 13, pp. 6-29, 2004.

Index